SIMPLE STEAM

by Debby Mitchell and Marnie Forestieri

Photography by Abel Gomez

Gryphon House

Lewisville, NC

Copyright
©2018 Debby Mitchell and Marnie Forestieri

Published by Gryphon House, Inc.
P. O. Box 10, Lewisville, NC 27023
800.638.0928; 877.638.7576 (fax)
Visit us on the web at www.gryphonhouse.com.
Library of Congress Cataloging-in-Publication Data
The cataloging-in-publication data is registered with the Library of Congress for ISBN 978-0-87659-752-1.

Bulk Purchase
Gryphon House books are available for special premiums and sales promotions as well as for fund-raising use. Special editions or book excerpts also can be created to specifications. For details, contact the director of marketing at Gryphon House.

Disclaimer
Gryphon House, Inc. cannot be held responsible for damage, mishap, or injury incurred during the use of or because of activities in this book. Appropriate and reasonable caution and adult supervision of children involved in activities and corresponding to the age and capability of each child involved are recommended at all times. Do not leave children unattended at any time. Observe safety and caution at all times.

Thank you to photographer Abel Gomez and to the families and staff members at Amazing Explorers Academy in Oviedo, Florida.

TABLE OF CONTENTS

INTRODUCTION

"Preschool years should be about play, joy, and fun."
—Dr. Deirdre Englehart

You bring a defenseless baby home, and in the blink of an eye your little one transforms into an active toddler, then a persistent preschooler, and ends up becoming a challenging teenager. Some of us enjoy the experience so much that we try it again and again just to realize that it doesn't get easier.

According to the National Scientific Council on the Developing Child at Harvard University, "An 'environment of relationships' is crucial for the development of a child's brain architecture, which lays the foundation for later outcomes such as academic performance, mental health, and interpersonal skills." Neuroscientific contributions translate into positive interactions and resources for parents and caregivers, and with more access to technology at an early age, babies' interests are becoming more sophisticated, the questions are getting harder, and they are more tech savvy! There is no way we will keep up if we don't go back to basics. We are raising children who will have careers that don't yet exist, spell words that are not yet in the dictionary, and be challenged to solve problems we don't even have.

So what can we do to raise children who are excited about the careers of the future? The focus of STEM (science, technology, engineering, and mathematics) or STEAM (science, technology, engineering, the arts, and mathematics) at all levels of education is becoming a popular trend. An increasing number of jobs at all levels require knowledge of STEAM.

For young children, this type of learning is active and fun! Yet, research documents that by the time students reach third grade, one third of boys and girls have lost interest in science. That means millions of students have dismissed these careers or lack the confidence to believe they can do science or math. A weak early childhood experience requires remedial strategies and other interventions that are more costly and less effective.

The Twenty-First Century Movement

Educating children for the careers of the future requires an understanding of the skills that employees need to succeed in the workplace: the twenty-first century skill movement. According to studies from the Programme for International Student Assessments, or PISA, school systems are not preparing students for the abilities and skills that build the foundation for lifelong learning such as problem solving, developing deeper understanding of subjects, or literacy.

The Conference Board, Corporate Voices for Working Families, Partnership for 21st Century Skills, and the Society for Human Resource Management surveyed over four hundred employers across the United States. In a final report, "Are They Really Ready to Work? Employers' Perspectives on the Basic Knowledge and Applied Skills of New Entrants to the 21st Century US Workforce," researchers identified four critical skills required by all employers regardless of the career:

- Creativity
- Communications
- Teamwork/Collaboration
- Critical Thinking/Problem Solving

The good news is that young children are wired with all of the critical skills of the twenty-first century.

Creativity

Young children are not afraid to express themselves and try new things through different mediums or forms of art. Practice makes perfect but does not inspire innovation or creativity. The arts allow children to become original thinkers as they take risks to express themselves in different ways and find joy in their work.

Researcher Karlyn Adams has found evidence that shows that creativity and innovation do not necessarily come from knowledge or experience, but instead derive from people being able to connect to originality, experience joy in their work, and have the passion to pursue a new idea. Adams finds that when students develop their passion, they are more confident and practice important skills such as persistence and risk taking.

Communication Building

Strong communication skills at an early age build a good foundation for future school years and for the rest of a child's life. At an early age, even a quiet child may have something to say when you connect to her. Communication skills are promoted when you build a child's confidence, encourage a child to find her own voice, and provide a variety of experiences to use descriptive words to promote understanding and communicate ideas. Using words, providing a literacy-rich environment, and offering books on STEAM topics provide young children with the tools for expressing their ideas.

Collaboration

Young children enjoy working together to solve a problem or talking with peers to find a solution. Peer-based work is easier with preschoolers as they are natural collaborators. Researcher Robert J. Sternberg has identified three main aspects that make up a positive learning environment: the creative, the analytical, and the practical. A successful learning environment allows children to generate ideas that are novel, lets children judge the value of their own ideas, and helps them understand their ideas as relevant to everyday contexts.

Furthermore, introducing young children to activities related to social and character development, such as empathy, composure, and choice, will allow children to understand the foundation of collaborating with others to achieve a higher purpose.

A gifted child without social skills rarely connects at all levels or comes up with innovations or fixes for problems. It takes a team of people to create something original, fix broken systems, or transform a nation. And to be a team player, children need to understand the rules of engaging and working with other team members.

Critical Thinking

Critical-thinking skills help us make decisions. These skills fully develop during adolescence, but the foundations of good thinking are rooted in early childhood experiences. When children are exposed to an environment that allows a child to value ideas, evaluate strengths and weaknesses, and think of ways to create solutions, they have opportunities to engage in the learning process, come up with solutions to problems, and connect to real-world situations.

Parents of young children value their children's natural abilities, the persistence to try things over and over, and the interest to research and discover ways to solve a problem. To make their own decisions, children must feel competent, be confident about those decisions, and consider the process of making decisions fun. Parents of young children are able to engage children in critical-thinking opportunities by setting expectations, allowing young children to make decisions, and encouraging children to express their preferences. Making choices builds children's sense of responsibility and ability to have an impact. Giving a toddler the option to choose between a crayon or tempera paint to produce art allows her to start making decisions for herself. To understand what inhibits critical-thinking skills, it is important to consider the environments or actions that might have a negative impact on a child's ability to make decisions. For example, environments or experiences that expose children to repetition without concrete experiences, such as worksheets, coloring-book pages, or adult-directed activities, inhibit a child's ability to make decisions or engage in the learning experience.

A Playful Approach to STEAM Learning

The components of a STEAM curriculum include the following:

- **Science** is the foundation of children's learning about their world and is also a way of thinking. Encouraging children to ask questions and to observe, predict, and explain their ideas supports the development of scientific inquiry. The skills and processes of inquiry, observation, and exploration are foundation skills for all sciences and are not limited to "science" time. Aligned with science, we integrate mathematics, arts, technology, and engineering activities as a general focus of this book.

- **Technology** for young children includes the integration of tools that are used to support children's work. Children enjoy building and creating things and are often intrigued with how stuff works. Technology is also finding out how things are constructed. Engaging your child in finding out what is inside objects such as old computers, TV sets, or toys promotes an interest in technology. Parents should be aware of the risks that come with loose parts in objects such as computers and toys, which may contain harmful substances. Make sure children are supervised at all times during activities that include taking things apart.

There is a common misconception that technology consists of only hardware, software, apps, or videos. *Technology* refers to a wide variety of tools used to acquire new knowledge, make work easier, or perform a job. These tools can range from simple crayons, scissors, and a clipboard to more sophisticated items like digital cameras and tablets. Software, videos, and other online resources are complementary to learning about a topic. Based on the premise that children at this age learn through concrete experiences and not abstract concepts, young children need to be able to manipulate concrete objects and not be recipients of information solely from a computer or TV screen. For a young child to be able to understand an abstract concept, she must be able to integrate experiences that engage all the senses.

- **Engineering** challenges children to use their creativity and practice critical-thinking skills by encouraging them to solve practical problems using technology tools to design something better. Challenging your children to design and create new things provides foundational skills that promote engineering concepts.

- **The Arts** are vital for engaging, inspiring, and promoting a sense of innovation. Research studies of programs using performing-arts strategies in the classroom provide evidence that the arts improve children's language and literacy skills and allow them to develop innovations, initiatives, social skills, and creative representations.

As schools and programs shift heavily to core subjects such as math or reading, there is a lack of awareness of the importance of the arts. When children produce art they are learning to take risks by expressing themselves and being original, skills needed to innovate across different subjects. Art disciplines include visual art, performance, music, dance, and so on. Integrating arts into other subjects helps children understand concepts more clearly.

- **Mathematics** often goes hand in hand with science and engineering as it gives children the language to share findings of investigations and problems. Foundational math skills include number sense, measurement, patterns and sequencing, and data analysis. Mathematics concepts are formed through concrete experiences and are embedded in all activities during the day.

Research indicates that when we engage younger children in the STEAM fields, we are promoting inquiry-based thinking and a discovery mentality. Teaching young children STEAM play is a way of teaching them how to research, think, and create as open-ended play becomes part of their early experiences. In addition to these benefits, introducing STEAM concepts using a multisensory approach and in a playful way gives young children a competitive advantage and sets a strong foundation for future study habits.

Before standardized testing begins and fun is no longer a priority, the foundational skills learned during the early years allow a child to feel confident about her abilities to do science, math, or engineering. Early experiences shape the way the brain functions and teach children a way of thinking and solving problems for life. Therefore, this wonderful window of opportunity during early childhood lays the foundation for brain development and may also lead to interest in STEAM careers.

You are probably asking yourself, how can I promote STEAM thinking without any prior experience, content knowledge, or teaching skills? Our model is very simple. It builds on your child's natural ability to play, her interest and curiosity to learn about the world, the persistence for trying new things, and the creativity to solve problems. When a young child begins to play, she asks questions such as "What would happen if I do this?" The model offers opportunities to learn through intentional playful activities and offers a facilitator's guide, vocabulary, key concepts, and guided questions. You can revisit the experiences through reflections that connect the experience to real-world problems. The activities in this book allow you and your child to acquire new knowledge and discover the joy of researching a topic, from making predictions to creating a project.

Time and Materials

The activities in this book can help children expand learning that naturally develops while playing with materials commonly found in most homes. Each activity allows you to engage with materials in intentional activities that will seem as though you both are simply playing together.

Introducing different materials will make things interesting. Review the activity and guided questions ahead of time, and have materials readily available. Allow children to explore the materials and engage in the experiences at their own pace. At a young age, children need time and encouragement to explore, investigate, and learn.

The Role of the Parent

The good news is that you don't have to be an expert, a researcher, or a scientist to get your child excited about STEAM careers and STEAM thinking. Remember, most STEAM learning is about exploring and learning from your exploration—so why not explore together? The main goal is not to make sure children master a concept, but simply to allow them to explore the activity in their own way. Giving this freedom to children inspires them to make predictions and critically think about the world around them in a pressure-free setting.

"Young children's learning reflects a cycle that begins with exploration with materials and then progresses as children develop concepts. This cycle of learning that occurs through explorations, inquiry and building of knowledge uses similar processes as the engineering method and scientific inquiry. It is important young children have time to observe and interact with materials during play. A variety of materials stimulate children's curiosity."

— Englehart et al., 2016

As a parent, you can encourage inquiry and curiosity by talking with your children about their questions and by interacting with them during the activities. Having conversations during mealtimes and providing feedback helps to promote their thinking and learning processes. Open-ended questions provide a rich context for engaging young children in meaningful conversations to enhance their learning.

By asking the right questions to get children thinking, you will begin an amazing journey that builds their confidence and understanding of the ways to discover new knowledge.

It's okay not to have all the answers or know all the subjects. If math, science, or engineering subjects seem intimidating, you may be reluctant to discover the subjects together with your child. So the process starts with you. When you change the mind-set, you start seeing your child in a different way and you become a partner, a facilitator, and a co-researcher.

The most critical skill for parents raising twenty-first century learners is to understand that you don't need to know all the answers. Our model allows you to introduce complicated STEAM subjects in a hands-on and fun way by following the activity format in our book. So, the next time your child asks a question you can't answer, incorporate a very helpful skill that we practice on a regular basis: "I don't know the answer; why don't we find out together?"

How to Use This Book

Each chapter is focused on a specific content area and includes twelve guided learning activities. The second portion of the book shares how to develop more activities using our format.

The goal of many activities is to support children's natural interests; many activities can be introduced while you are reading to your child during breakfast or at some other convenient time. Some activities require you to be more focused or involved with your children, while others allow more flexibility and playtime.

Prepare the Activity

The first paragraph of the activity gives you an overview of the activity's learning goals and key concepts.
Prior to starting an activity, check the "What You Need" list to prepare the experience and gather the materials required. The "Talk Like an Expert" section gives you terms and definitions that will lead to more learning and rich vocabulary and communication as you do the activity with your child.

Develop the Activity

During an activity, assist, question, interact, or observe your child as needed during intentional play.

We suggest that you introduce one activity per day in different domains using the directions provided. This will help to create excitement about specific concepts and will allow you to maintain a focus on the learning goal for the day. Introduce the subject by asking your child a question or by sparking their curiosity.

In the "How to Do It" section, we offer questions you can ask to guide your child's thinking. These questions will start a conversation and engage your child in a discussion to help you understand what he knows about the topic. An important part of the process is to listen to your child's ideas and not interrupt them. At this point, guiding the process of learning is not about answering a question but about allowing your child to find the answer on his own. If needed, or if your child is interested in learning more, look up images or videos about the subject.

Read the directions aloud for your child, and collaborate as you discuss and plan how to conduct the learning experience. Your child will have the opportunity to predict and create a project in a hands-on way. Do the activity together.

When you've completed the exploration, use some of the ideas in the "Predict and Hypothesize" section to explore more ways to do the activity. This will allow your child to think creatively and consider how to redesign the experience if needed. Create a hands-on project together.

At the end of each activity, examples are provided in the "Add more STEAM activities" section to integrate the different domains and enrich the experience.

Reflections

At the end of every activity, encourage your child to share her findings with the rest of the family. Taking pictures during the activity will allow you to share the experience and engage everyone. At a later time, perhaps during dinner or when the family is together, revisit the experience. Ask your child to share what she has learned. Some activities suggest that children share their work with the rest of the family to start a conversation. The children will take pride and satisfaction with their work, and this is a way of making the learning process visible for the child and the family.

PART 1

SCIENCE

Parachutes ❯

Explore the concepts of air resistance, gravity, force, and mass by making a parachute with your child!

 Talk Like Scientists!

Discussing these terms may lead to more learning and rich vocabulary and communication.

- **Air resistance**—a pushing force that slows things down
- **Force**—a push or pull on an object; for example, how hard you throw your parachute into the air
- **Gravity**—a force that pulls things toward the earth; it keeps you on the ground so you do not float
- **Mass**—a measurement of how much matter is in an object; for example, an object's weight

What You Need

- Plastic grocery bags (If a plastic bag is not available you can use tissue paper, a coffee filter, or newspaper). Another option is to punch holes in corners of a plastic container with a lid. With a plastic container, you can change the items in the container, and thus change the weight. You can see how different weights affect the parachute.
- Something to weigh down the bag (toy, rock, etc.)
- String or yarn
- Scissors
- STEAM journal (notebook to record observations)

How to Do It

1. Spark curiosity by asking your child, "What is a parachute? Why do people use them?"
2. Listen to your child's ideas and talk about them. If needed, or if your child is interested in learning more, look up images or videos of parachutes online. Talk with your child about what you notice about the parachutes. Continue to communicate and ask questions throughout the activity.
3. Collaborate with your child to make a homemade parachute. Use a plastic grocery bag. ⚠ **Safety Note: Always keep a close eye on young children when they are using plastic bags as they are a choking hazard.** If a plastic bag is not available you can use tissue paper, a coffee filter, or newspaper. The reason a plastic bag may be preferable is that you can squish and ball it up to make a good throw in the air.
4. Cut the handles of the bag so you have four areas to tie your string onto the plastic.
5. Tie a length of string or yarn to the cut handles of your plastic bag. String can be 8 to 15 inches long, depending on size of bag. Now you should have four equal strings hanging from the parachute.
6. Bring the four loose pieces together with equal lengths.
7. Tie the four strings to an object with weight (toy, rock, or other item). Another option is to punch holes in four corners of a plastic container with a lid so you change out the weighted items as you wish.
8. Throw the parachute!
9. Encourage your child's curiosity: I wonder if it will make a difference if we throw it soft or hard. Does it matter if we ball up the parachute before throwing? If we throw a plastic bag in the air without any weight, I wonder what would happen.
10. Encourage your child's critical-thinking skills: What can you tell me about making a parachute?

Predict and Hypothesize

- Problem solve with your child: I wonder what will happen if we add different weighted objects.
- Try tying different objects to the parachute, and predict and make a hypothesis about what will happen. What objects could you tie to the parachute or put into the container? Test the hypothesis by using different objects of different weights. Chart what you discover.

Add more STEAM activities:

Technology—Use a stopwatch to see how long the parachute takes to reach the ground, or make a video of the different tosses to analyze later.

Engineering—Discuss, plan, and draw how you will design and build your parachute.

Arts—Draw/paint a parachute or create a parachute dance.

Math—Weigh objects suspended by the parachute (or in the container), chart how many seconds the parachute floats, and talk about what you notice.

What You Should Be Seeing

You may see some unsuccessful attempts in the parachute opening, which is a great opportunity to talk about what is happening. If the parachute is not tossed high enough (with enough force) it may not get enough air resistance to open. Some materials will open easier than other materials. Sometimes the wind will carry the parachute. You will also note that the weight has to be enough for the parachute to glide smoothly. If the weight is too little or too much, you can see the effect on the parachute and then discuss gravity and mass.

Rain Clouds 〉

Explore a rain cloud by simulating the concept using shaving cream and food coloring.

 Talk Like Scientists!

- **Cloud**—a white or gray mass in the sky that is made of many very small drops of water
- **Precipitation**—a deposit on the earth of hail, mist, rain, sleet, or snow
- **Rain cloud**—a cloud (as a nimbus) bringing rain
- **Saturated**—full of moisture; made thoroughly wet

What You Need

- Shaving foam
- Glasses or vase (clear and large enough to use for container for experiment)
- Jars or small bowls (small enough to hold a few ounces of food coloring)
- Food coloring
- Measuring spoons
- Measuring cup
- Water
- STEAM journal

How to Do It

1. Ask your child, "What is a rain cloud?" "How do you know when it is going to rain?"
2. Talk with your child about the different types of rain clouds.
3. Fill each of the smaller jars with 1 ounce of water and 10 drops of food coloring. You may have only one jar with one color or you may want to have different jars that each have a different color. Note that purple may need only a few drops of food coloring.
4. Fill a clear container 2/3 full of water and top it liberally with shaving cream.
5. Use the small measuring spoon to drop the single color (or different colors) of colored water from the smaller jars into the shaving cream cloud.

6. Discuss that in this experiment the clear water in the bowl is like the air and the shaving cream is like the clouds. The shaving cream clouds will become so saturated with the food coloring that it will "rain."

7. Encourage your child's curiosity: I wonder what it will look like if we use only one color. I wonder how long it takes to see the rain in our experiment.

8. Encourage your child's critical-thinking skills: What can you tell me about making rain clouds in this experiment? What could we do differently in this experiment?

Predict and Hypothesize

- Problem solve with your child: How are different colors made? I wonder what will happen if we use more than one color.
- Try using different color combinations in new containers with shaving cream to see what happens. Predict what will happen and make a hypothesis.

Add more STEAM activities:

Technology—Use a stopwatch to see how long it takes for the "rain" to occur.

Engineering—Discuss what inventions, machines, and structures protect us from the rain, sleet, and snow.

Arts—Use this opportunity to combine different colors and note how, when colors are combined, they make a "new" color. Example: Combining yellow and red will make orange. Draw or paint pictures with rain clouds and/or make up a rain dance.

Math—Measure the amount of food coloring being combined. Note what will happen if more shaving cream or more color is added. Use a rain collector to collect and chart actual rainfall.

What You Should Be Seeing

You may see shades of colors that are slightly different from the colors you thought you would see due to the amount of food coloring and how they mix together. This is a good opportunity to add more food coloring and discuss color variations. If the layer of shaving cream is too thick it will take longer and may become boring. Using less water will give you a faster reaction. Using more water will make the rain "fall" longer.

Anemometer 〉

Learn how to make an anemometer by making a device that uses cuplike shapes to catch the wind, causing the device to spin. How many times it spins in a given time period can tell you how fast the wind is moving.

 Talk Like Scientists!

- **Anemometer**—an instrument for measuring and indicating the force or speed and direction of the wind
- **Speed**—rate of motion, or how fast something is moving
- **Weather**—the state of the atmosphere with respect to heat or cold, wetness or dryness, calm or storm, clearness or cloudiness
- **Wind**—a natural movement of air of any velocity
- **Wind speed**—how fast air is moving

What You Need

- 5 small paper cups
- 2 straws
- Hole punch
- Scissors
- Tape
- Stapler (optional)
- Marker
- Pencil with eraser
- Pushpin
- Plastic container with lid
- Weight heavy enough to hold container in place (rocks, tools, dirt)
- Stopwatch
- STEAM journal

How to Do It

1. Ask your child, "What can you tell me about the wind and the weather outside?" Discuss sun, rain, wind, and clouds. "When is wind needed?" "What can happen if there is too much wind?"

2. Discuss your child's ideas and, if she's interested, look up images or videos of wind in weather reports or how wind impacts sailboats, kites, etc. Talk with your child about the power of wind. Continue to ask questions throughout the activity.

3. Punch a hole in four of the cups about a centimeter (0.39 inches) down from the rim.

4. In the fifth cup punch four evenly spaced holes about a centimeter (0.39 inches) down from the rim. Also punch a small hole in the bottom center of this cup.

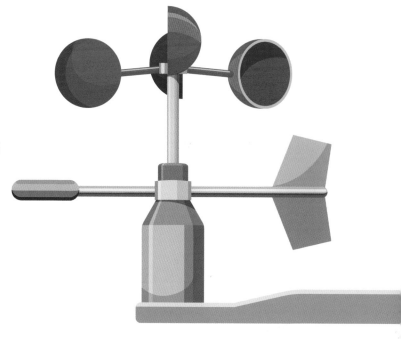

5. Make a small hole in the center of the lid of the plastic container.

6. Push a pencil through the center hole of the fifth cup and also through the plastic cover of the container. This will be the center of the anemometer.

7. Weigh down the container by adding some type of weight (sand, tools, rocks) so the wind will not knock over the anemometer.

8. Slide one of the straws through the hole in one of the four cups that has only one hole in it. Bend the end of the straw that is inside the cup and tape or staple it to the inside of the cup.

9. Place the other end of the straw through two of the holes in the fifth cup, then through the hole in one of the other cups. Also tape or staple the end of the straw to the inside of the cup.

10. Repeat the last two steps with the remaining two cups.

11. Make sure the four cups all have their open ends facing in the same direction (clockwise) around the center cup and pencil.

12. Push the pushpin through the two straws where they overlap and then into the pencil eraser (make sure it's not too tight—you want straws to be able to turn). The pushpin will be your rotation axis.

13. Mark one of the cups with a marker. Use that cup as your starting point when measuring wind speed.

14. Test the anemometer without anything tied to it. Encourage your child's curiosity: I wonder how many times the cups will turn in one full circle in a minute. I wonder if it will make a difference if the wind is blowing soft or hard.

15. Encourage your child's critical-thinking skills: What can you tell me about making an anemometer? What would we do differently if we made another anemometer?

Predict and Hypothesize

- Problem solve with your child: Will it make a difference if we place the anemometer in different places in our yard (where wind is blocked or not blocked)? Does the wind speed change during the day?
- Move the anemometer to different locations and create a schedule for morning and afternoon to check the wind.
- Predict and hypothesize the answers to the questions. Test the hypothesis and chart what you discover.

Add more STEAM activities:

Technology—Use a stopwatch to count how many times your marked cup goes by for one minute.

Engineering—Discuss, plan, and draw how you will design and build your anemometer.

Arts—Draw/paint scenes where wind is needed. Play music and pretend to be leaves floating or swirling in the wind.

Math—Measure (count) and record the wind speed two or three times a day or week and chart/graph the data. Compare wind in the morning to wind in the afternoon.

What You Should Be Seeing

If the pushpin is too tight, your straws may not turn. Take your time to measure the locations of the holes in the cups to insert straws. Make sure the axis is placed in the center of the crossed straws to ensure balance. Don't be surprised if you don't have enough wind to turn the anemometer. If necessary, use an electric fan to demonstrate.

Seed Investigations 》

Explore the difference between fruits and vegetables by conducting a seed investigation with your child. Visit your local farmers' market or grocery store to find different types of fruits and vegetables.

What You Need

- Clipboard
- Old magazines
- Paper
- Pencil
- Scavenger hunt sheet with fruits and vegetables
- *Muncha! Muncha! Muncha!* by Candace Fleming (optional)
- STEAM journal

 Talk Like Scientists!

- **Embryo**—a tiny young plant inside a seed
- **Fruit**—the usually edible reproductive body of a seed plant
- **Germinate**—to cause to sprout or develop
- **Life cycle**—a seed will sprout and produce a small plant called a seedling, which will grow to form a mature plant that will then reproduce by forming new seeds
- **Parts of the plant**—the stem supports the plant, the leaves make food for the plant, the fruits hold and protect the seeds
- **Seed**—the fertilized ripened ovule of a flowering plant containing an embryo and normally capable of germination to produce a new plant
- **Vegetable**—a usually herbaceous plant (such as the cabbage, bean, or potato) grown for an edible part that is usually eaten as part of a meal

How to Do It

1. Ask your child, "What is the difference between fruits and vegetables?"
2. Listen to your child's ideas and write them in your science journal. Tell your child that you will both discover the answer together upon your visit to the farmers' market or grocery store. Make sure not to answer the question at this point, as it will be a great learning experience for your child to find the answer to the question after the activity.
3. Begin your seed investigation. Explain to your child that you will be playing a special game called a scavenger hunt.
4. Give your child the clipboard and the scavenger hunt sheet with the fruits and vegetables to

search for during your visit to the farmers' market or grocery store.

5. Once you have found an item, encourage your child to mark it off. If possible, buy the item to explore further at home.
6. Once you have completed the activity, ask her how many items were collected.
7. Invite your child to count the items one by one.
8. Allow your child to observe and explore a fruit and a vegetable and compare the items.
9. Encourage your child's curiosity: I wonder if our fruits and vegetables are soft or hard. I wonder how we can tell if a fruit or vegetable is ready to eat or it has to be cooked.
10. Encourage your child's critical-thinking skills: What can you tell me about fruits and vegetables?
11. Encourage your child's communication skills by sharing your discoveries at dinner with the rest of the family, or at any time when everyone is together. What an exciting and fun way for children to learn!

Predict and Hypothesize

- Problem solve with your child: How we can sort and tell the difference between fruits and vegetables?
- If your child understands the difference, allow him to sort the fruits and vegetables.
- Test your hypothesis by cutting open the fruit and allowing your child to observe the seeds inside. Ask him if the vegetable has seeds.

Add more STEAM activities:

Technology—Use a story kit app to retell the life cycle of the plant.

Engineering—Use the book *Muncha! Muncha! Muncha!* by Candice Fleming as a reference to help Mr. McGreely find a solution to keep the rabbits away from his garden. Engage your child in a discussion of possible solutions.

Arts—Cut pictures of fruits and vegetables from old magazines and make your own scavenger hunt sheet.

Math—Practice one-on-one correspondence by inviting your child to count and sort fruits and vegetables in the market.

What You Should Be Seeing

Children may struggle to understand the differences between fruits and vegetables. You may choose to sort in other ways such as color or size. You can measure the circumference of the fruits or vegetables and use it as an additional math activity.

Worm Habitats ❯

In this activity, you and your child will explore and learn more about worms, what they eat, and why compost is good for our gardens. After the experiment, make sure to release the worms back into the wild.

 Talk Like Scientists!

- **Compost**—a mixture that consists largely of decayed organic matter and is used for fertilizing and conditioning soil
- **Fertilizer**—a substance (such as manure or a chemical mixture) used to make soil more fertile
- **Plant**—a young tree, vine, shrub, or herb
- **Soil**—the upper layer of earth that may be dug or plowed and in which plants grow
- **Worm**—any of numerous relatively small, elongated invertebrate, and soft-bodied animals

What You Need

- Earthworms
- Tray
- Black construction paper
- White paper
- Magnifying glass
- Clear jar or container with a lid (small holes should be punched in lid so worms can get oxygen)
- Dirt
- Sand
- Spray bottle with water
- Carrots, lettuce, coffee grounds, small pieces of shredded newspaper
- STEAM journal

How to Do It

1. Begin by asking your child, "Have you ever seen a worm?" "Do you think worms have legs and arms?" "Where do worms live and what do they do all day?" "Tell me what you know about worms."
2. Listen to your child's comments and engage her in a conversation about why worms are important for gardening.
3. Give your child a tray with sand and dirt inside and go dig outdoors to find worms. You can also purchase worms at a bait shop.

4. Invite your child to observe the worms and record observations in a science journal. Remind her that she does not need to touch the worms at all and that her job is to notice how they move around the soil.
5. Ask your child, "Can you see any eyes?" Put the worms on a tray to observe. Ask, "Do they have legs or arms?"
6. Invite your child to draw a picture of the worm in the science journal.
7. Have your child look at the worms through a magnifying glass and investigate how they move.
8. Once the worms burrow under the dirt, add some food to the container (carrots, lettuce, coffee grounds, and shredded newspaper). You may want to add food in isolated small sections on top to notice what happens.
9. Place a piece of black construction paper around the container to make it dark inside, to simulate being underground. Make it easy to remove the covering so you can periodically view the worms.
10. Spray the habitat every few days to keep it damp (but not too wet!). Add more food as needed.

11. Encourage discussion and help your child develop a hypothesis about what the worms will do in their new habitat.
12. Once you're finished with the activity, make sure to release the worms back into the wild.
13. Encourage your child's critical-thinking skills: What can you tell me about worms? Were we successful making our worm habitat? What is the job of a worm?

Predict and Hypothesize

- Problem solve with your child: I wonder what else worms might eat. What happens to a banana after it is rotten? Do you think the worms will eat it?
- Tell your child that worms like to eat some of the same foods we eat, but they like to eat it when the food is rotten (food that is old and decayed). Feed the worms in the container some rotten food for the experiment. Explain that after worms finish eating, they turn food into compost.
- Test the hypothesis by looking periodically at the worms and making notes about what you see. You could also try white paper on one side of the container and black on the other side to see what happens. Usually the worms will move toward the black paper, mix up the dirt and sand, and make tunnels.

Add more STEAM activities:

Technology—Use a stopwatch to conduct an experiment about a worm's favorite color (white or dark paper). Take daily pictures of the worms and their container, then journal about what you see.

Engineering—Design and build a new worm habitat.

Arts—Draw a worm and its habitat. Make up a dance about dancing worms wiggling into the ground.

Math—Measure worms or count how many you can see on the white- or black-covered side and record your observations in your science journal.

What You Should Be Seeing

You may have difficulty seeing the worms. Make sure the jar diameter is not too wide so worms can easily be seen. Often, children do not note the changes, so take time to discuss what you saw the previous time compared to each time you observe. Make sure not to add too much food or water—so the jar does not get smelly—and yet enough that the worms have adequate food.

Sorting Trash/Garbage ❯

Much of the trash we throw away could be recycled, reused, or composted. Instead, it winds up in a landfill, where some garbage takes a long time to decompose, damaging our environment. Discuss with your child how recycling, reusing, and composting can benefit people and our Earth.

What You Need
- Plastic bins
- Snack/picnic foods, plates, and containers
- STEAM journal

Talk Like Scientists!

- **Compost**—a mixture that consists largely of decayed organic matter and is used for fertilizing and conditioning soil
- **Decompose**—to cause something (such as dead plants) to be slowly destroyed and broken down by natural processes
- **Environment**—the surrounding conditions or forces (such as soil, climate, and living things) that influence a plant's or animal's characteristics and ability to survive
- **Fertilizer**—a substance (such as manure or a chemical mixture) used to make soil more fertile
- **Inorganic**—being or composed of matter other than plant or animal
- **Landfill**—a system of trash and garbage disposal in which the waste is buried between layers of earth to build up low-lying land
- **Organic**—of, relating to, or obtained from living things
- **Recycle**—to reuse or make a substance available for reuse
- **Waste**—of, relating to, or being material that is left over or unwanted after something has been made, done or used

How to Do It

1. Start a conversation with your child about keeping our world and environment healthy. Ask, "What is trash?" "Can you name things that you throw in the trash?" "What do you think happens once the trash leaves our house?" "Do you know what it means to recycle?" If you have recycling bins, ask, "What types of things do we put in the recycle bin?" "Can some of the items we throw in our trash be reused here in our own home?" Examples: a container, an old toothbrush to use for cleaning, and so on.
2. To learn more, look up images or videos of trash, recycling, composting, and landfills.
3. With your child, you can sort trash by going for a picnic or having a snack.
4. Make sure to have a variety of "trash" items. After eating, have your child sort different items into bins to recycle (paper, plastic, metal, rubber), reuse (container), or compost (organic items).
5. If you do not have recycling, look for a store that recycles to take the items to donate.
6. If you do not have a compost area, use a small portion in the yard or make a small box (lined with plastic) filled with soil to use as a compost area.
7. Place several different trash items (organic, such as a banana peel, and inorganic, such as a plastic container) into the compost area. Conduct an investigation into the process of decomposition by recording your child's observations. Encourage discussion and invite your child to make a hypothesis and predict what will happen to the trash in the compost area.
8. Encourage your child's critical-thinking skills: What can you tell me about trash? Were we successful in sorting our trash? What can you tell me about making a compost area? Why is it important to make good decisions with our trash?

Predict and Hypothesize

- Problem solve with your child: I wonder what would happen if we left a banana, newspaper, and a plastic cup out in our compost area. I wonder why the banana is turning dark. What is causing the smell?
- Test the hypothesis by looking periodically at the items in the compost area. Chart your results.

What You Should Be Seeing

Sometimes it may take a little while to see the results from your compost area, but don't forget about it and check it frequently. After a time you will see lots of interesting bugs, worms, and flies in that area, especially if you turn the soil. You can then discuss the importance of each of those in the process of decomposition.

Technology—Take pictures to document the decomposition of the banana or other foods.

Engineering/Art—Design and build an art project using recycled materials.

Math—Predict about how long it will take for a banana to decompose and for a can to decompose. Record the predictions on paper, and then compare at the end of the week and month.

Dancing Worms 》

Explore the science behind a chemical reaction that will cause worms to appear to dance!

 Talk Like Scientists!

- **Chemical reaction**—a change that occurs when two or more substances combine to form a new substance
- **Mixture**—a portion of matter consisting of two or more components in varying proportions that retain their own properties

What You Need

- 2 clear glasses
- Sharp knife (adult use only)
- Cutting board
- Gummy worms
- Baking soda
- Warm water
- Vinegar
- Fork or tongs
- Timer
- STEAM journal

How to Do It

1. Engage your child's curiosity by asking her about examples we find in our everyday life that are caused by a chemical reaction. "What do you think causes something to rust?" "What do you think happens to make something rot and get smelly?" "What causes an egg to be cooked and look differently?" It is a hard concept to understand, but those things were caused by a chemical reaction. Tell your child that you are going to make gummy worms dance by mixing different things together that will cause a chemical reaction.

2. If your child is interested in learning more, there are many great resources for watching chemical reactions online. This is a complex concept, so many children, especially the youngest ones, will just be excited about seeing the reaction of the gummy worms dancing.

3. Cut a gummy worm into four parts. A wet knife might make it easier to cut.

4. Measure 3 tablespoons of baking soda and stir into 1 cup of warm water. Place the four cut pieces of gummy worms into the water. Set a timer for fifteen minutes so the worms have time to soak up the baking soda mixture.

5. While waiting, fill the second glass with a cup of vinegar.

6. The mixture will start forming bubbles and the gummy worms will start "dancing" immediately. This chemical reaction is due to the acid in the vinegar reacting to the bicarbonate in the baking soda, which forms gas bubbles that will lift the worms up. Once the baking soda has been used in the process, the bubbles will stop forming.

7. Encourage your child's curiosity: Do you think the gummy worms would "dance" if we put them in regular water?

8. Encourage your child's critical-thinking skills: Can you tell me about the substances we combined together to make a mixture? Why do you think the gummy worms stopped dancing? What can you tell me about the dancing gummy worms?

Predict and Hypothesize

- Problem solve with your child: I wonder what would happen if we put more gummy worms into the mixture. I wonder how long the worms will move. Predict and make a hypothesis about what will happen.
- Test the hypothesis by adding more gummy worms. You could use a timer to help chart what you discover.

What You Should Be Seeing

If your worms are not dancing, it may be that you did not wait enough time for the worms to soak up the baking soda, the water is not warm enough, or there are too many worms in the glass at one time.

Add more STEAM activities:

Technology—Make a video of the gummy worm dancing and put it to music.
Engineering—Discuss, plan, and draw a picture of a new container design.
Arts—Make up a wiggling worm dance!
Math—Make a chart of how long the gummy worms danced.

Sound Waves >

Explore sound waves and how they travel through the air. Children will also learn about the concepts of pitch, volume, and vibration.

What You Need

- Paper for chart
- Ruler (wood or heavy plastic)
- Spoons in a variety of sizes
- 3 to 4 feet of yarn
- STEAM journal

 Talk Like Scientists!

- **Conductor**—a material or object that allows electricity or heat to move through it
- **Pitch**—highness or lowness of sound
- **Reverberate**—to continue in a series of quickly repeated sounds that bounce off a surface (such as a wall)
- **Sound**—the sensation perceived by the sense of hearing
- **Sound waves**—formed when a sound (vibration) is made and moves through the air causing movement in the air particles. These particles bump into the particles close to them, which makes them vibrate too, causing them to bump into more air particles. This movement, called sound waves, keeps going until they run out of energy.
- **Vibration**—a series of small, fast movements back and forth or from side to side
- **Volume**—loudness or softness of sound

How to Do It

1. Spark your child's interest by asking, "What do you think would happen if I take this piece of paper and 'wave' it in the air?" "Do you hear the sound?" "How do you think sound travels from the paper to your ears?" Talk about how when noise or a sound is made, it creates sound waves that travel through the air and to our ears. Also discuss how sound is made by vibration. Ask your child to put her fingers on her neck while talking and making different sounds. Ask, "Do you feel the vibration?"
2. Discuss your child's ideas about sound, and research with her online if she is interested in learning more about sound waves.
3. Take the piece of yarn and find the middle.
4. Create a loop and insert the handle of a spoon.
5. Pull the yarn tightly to hold the spoon.
6. The spoon should hang in the center of the yarn of which you should have two long pieces of approximately equal length.
7. Take one length of yarn and have your child wrap it around her pointer finger on one hand, then repeat with the other length of yarn on her other hand so the spoon will hang in the middle of the string. The spoon should hang just below the waist of the child once both hands are placed near the ears.
8. Have your child push the string against each ear. (Note: String should not go into the ear but just outside as if you are going to plug your ears.)
9. Once the string is pushed against the ears, very lightly hit the ruler against the round part (the bowl) of the spoon.

10. Ask your child, "Did you hear anything?" She should hear a distinct sound. Discuss that the sound is caused by sound waves vibrating and moving (being conducted) up the yarn.
11. Encourage your child's curiosity: I wonder if it will make a difference if we tap the spoon soft or hard.
12. Encourage your child's critical-thinking skills: What can you tell me about sound waves?

Predict and Hypothesize

- Problem solve with your child: I wonder if we use a bigger or smaller spoon if it will change the sound. I wonder if we shorten the yarn if it will change the sound.
- Try different spoons and lengths and predict and make a hypothesis about what will happen.
- Test the hypothesis by using different lengths and sizes. Chart what you discover.

What You Should Be Seeing
Children may have a hard time distinguishing between the actual immediate sound versus the sound waves moving up the string. If so, vary even more the force used on the spoon.

Add more STEAM activities:

Technology—Use music apps to make your own music.

Engineering—Discuss, plan, and draw different types of instruments you could make.

Arts—Make your own instruments by using a shoe box and other size boxes and use different types of rubber bands to cause sound and vibration.

Math—Play music and keep it at the same volume. Measure how far you can move away from the source until you can't hear the sound anymore.

Elephant Toothpaste 》

Explore making a foamy substance caused by the rapid decomposition of hydrogen peroxide. This experiment creates an exothermic reaction—not only does it create foam, it also creates heat.

 Talk Like Scientists!

- **Bubble**—a sphere enclosing a small body of gas
- **Catalyst**—a substance that enables a chemical reaction to proceed at a faster rate or under different conditions (as at a lower temperature) than otherwise possible
- **Decompose**—to break up into constituent parts by or as if by a chemical process
- **Foam**—a light frothy mass of fine bubbles formed in or on the surface of a liquid or from a liquid
- **Gas**—a fluid (such as air) that has neither independent shape nor volume but tends to expand indefinitely
- **Heat**—added energy that causes substances to rise in temperature, fuse, evaporate, expand, or undergo any of various other related changes

What You Need
- Large soda bottle
- Small cup
- Pan or tray with high sides
- Measuring spoons
- Warm water
- Dry yeast
- Hydrogen peroxide (3 percent or 6 percent solution, can be found at a beauty supply store)
- Measuring cup
- Dish detergent
- Funnel
- Safety goggles
- Food coloring
- Timer
- STEAM journal

How to Do It

1. Engage your child by asking, "What do you think causes foam or bubbles?" "Where do you see foam or bubbles?"
2. Listen to your child's ideas and talk about things that make foam. You may want to look up images or videos online if she is curious to see other types of exothermic reactions.
3. Prepare your materials to make elephant toothpaste. Make sure to wear safety goggles any time you are mixing the ingredients.
4. In a small cup, add 3 tablespoons of warm water and 1 teaspoon of yeast. Important: Set aside and leave for at least three minutes (set the timer). You will notice some foam in the cup, which indicates that the yeast has been activated.

5. Set a plastic soda bottle in the middle of a pan or tray that will catch the spillover from the toothpaste.
6. Add 1/2 cup of hydrogen peroxide to the large soda bottle.
7. Add food coloring (approximately 8 to 10 drops) and approximately 1 tablespoon of dish detergent to the soda bottle. Carefully swish all ingredients around in the bottle.
8. Use a funnel and pour the yeast mixture into the soda bottle (which is the catalyst to make the hydrogen peroxide decompose or break down).
9. Step back and watch the foam bubbles gush out of the bottle. This is the oxygen becoming a gas due to the decomposition of the hydrogen peroxide.
10. Encourage your child's curiosity: Why do you think this experiment is called elephant toothpaste?
11. Encourage your child's critical-thinking skills: What can you tell me about elephant toothpaste and chemical reactions?

Predict and Hypothesize

- Problem solve with your child: I wonder what would happen if we tried different containers in which the "neck" was bigger or smaller.
- Try a few types of containers and predict and make a hypothesis about what will happen.
- Test the hypothesis by using different bottle neck sizes. Chart what you discover.

Add more STEAM activities:

Technology—Use a stopwatch to see how long the experiment continues to foam, or make a video.

Engineering—Discuss, plan, and draw different types of containers.

Arts—Make up an elephant toothpaste dance.

Math—Measure the neck circumference of the bottles and chart foaming results.

What You Should Be Seeing

The reaction you are seeing is called an exothermic reaction. It not only creates foam, it also creates heat. Each tiny foam bubble is filled with oxygen. The yeast acts as a catalyst to remove the oxygen from the hydrogen peroxide. The toothpaste is caused by the rapid decomposition of the hydrogen peroxide.

From Seed to Plant ❯

Seeds are living things that need water and nutrients to reproduce. In this activity, children will use lima bean seeds to learn about the life cycle of a seed.

What You Need

- Jars or cups
- Soil
- Lima bean seeds
- Water
- Magnifying glass
- Paper towel
- Pencil
- STEAM journal

 Talk Like Scientists!

- **Embryo**—a tiny young plant inside a seed
- **Germinate**—to cause to begin to grow
- **Seed**—the fertilized ripened ovule of a flowering plant containing an embryo and normally capable of germination to produce a new plant
- **Seed coat**—an outer protective covering of a seed

How to Do It

1. While looking at seeds with your child, ask, "What do you think the job of a seed is?" Tell your child that seeds come in many shapes and sizes. Some are little and some are big. But all seeds need the same things to grow into a plant. "What do you think seeds need to become a plant?" Tell your child that you will discover the answer together by conducting an experiment with lima bean seeds. Make sure not to answer the questions at this point, as it will be a great learning experience for your child to find the answer to the question after the activity.

2. Give your child a magnifying glass to investigate the bean seeds. Record the observations in the STEAM journal.

3. Place half of the lima beans in a jar and submerge them overnight in water. Soaking the beans will make them easier to examine.

4. On the following day, invite your child to open the seeds that were submerged in water and investigate what is inside. Open the seed and make observations about your findings. Ask, "Do you see a baby plant?" That is the embryo, a little plant inside the seed. Identify the different parts of the seed, including the seed coat and the embryo.

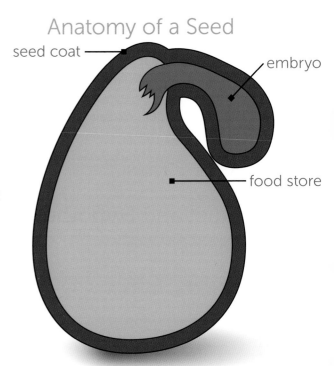

Anatomy of a Seed

seed coat

embryo

food store

5. Encourage your child's curiosity: I wonder if it will make a difference when we examine some of the lima beans that were not soaked in water.

6. Encourage your child's critical-thinking skills: What can you tell me about the inside of lima beans?

Predict and Hypothesize

- Problem solve with your child: I wonder what the little plant inside the seed (the embryo) needs to grow. Ask, "What do you think it needs?" "Do you think it will grow without water and soil?"
- Encourage your child to conduct an experiment to find the answer. Place some lima beans in a paper towel and do not water them for a week to test the hypothesis. Give your child some lima beans and have her place them into the cup that has soil and gets sunlight. Water the lima beans on a daily basis for a week.
- Test the hypothesis by using no water, a little water, and a lot of water and record the information. Chart what you discover.

Add more STEAM activities:

Technology—Take pictures to document the growth process from seed to plant.

Engineering—Invent a machine to disperse seeds.

Arts—Create an art project with seeds or make up a seed to plant dance.

Math—Count seeds and sort them. Begin by giving your child a magnifying glass to investigate. Measure beans before soaking them in water and record the results in your STEAM journal. Leave some beans overnight and measure them the following day. Ask your child guided questions: Why do you think soaked beans look different? What happened to the coat? Why do you think the lima bean is bigger after we put them in water?

What You Should Be Seeing
If your seeds split or rot, you may have soaked them in water too long.

Leaf Investigations 〉

Leaves come in all sorts of shapes and sizes. Gain an understanding of what leaves have in common and what makes them different. Leaves might look different but all leaves have the same job: to make food. Find out what leaves need to make food with an easy experiment.

 Talk Like Scientists!

- **Bark**—the tough exterior covering of a woody root or stem
- **Photosynthesis**—the process by which a green plant turns water and carbon dioxide into food when the plant is exposed to light
- **Roots**—parts of a plant that carry water and nutrients to the plant and support the plant
- **Tree**—a woody perennial plant having a single, main stem, generally with few or no branches on its lower part
- **Trunk**—the main stem of a tree apart from limbs and roots

What You Need

- Leaves (different shapes and sizes)
- Camera
- Water
- Measuring tools (rulers, Unifix cubes)
- Plants
- Black bag for cover so plant will not get sunlight
- Plastic bags for bringing leaves and other items home
- STEAM journal

How to Do It

1. Go outside with your child and ask, "What can you tell me about trees?" "What can you tell me about leaves?"
2. Listen to your child's ideas and discuss them. Examine a tree up close and record your child's observations about leaves and trees. Talk with your child about what you notice about the different parts of a tree.
3. With your child, collect leaves from different kinds of trees of different shapes and colors.
4. Bring the collection inside, make comparisons about what you observe, and find same and different characteristics such as size, color, and texture.

5. Encourage your child's curiosity: How are the leaves different or the same? What do you think they have in common?
6. Encourage your child's critical-thinking skills: What can you tell me about leaves?
7. Tell your child that regardless of their shape or size, all leaves have the same job. Leaves must make food for the plant.

Predict and Hypothesize

- Problem solve with your child: I wonder what plants need to make food. I wonder what will happen if we have two plants and keep one in a dark area and one that has sunlight.
- Find two plants to conduct the investigation. Move one plant to a dark room with no light. Place the other plant in sunlight. Continue to water both plants the same amount every few days.
- Test the hypothesis and record observations or document the experiment with a camera every few days. Chart what you discover. Ask, "What part of the plant needs to find sunlight?"

Add more STEAM activities:

Technology—Take pictures every few days of plant growth. Take pictures outside of leaves and document how they are different.

Engineering—Invent a machine or method to collect leaves in the fall.

Arts—Make an art project with leaves. Create a leaf rubbing by placing a leaf bottom-side up on a flat surface. Put a thin sheet of paper on top of the leaf and rub the paper with crayon or an oil pastel gently on the area over the leaf.

Math—Measure leaf sizes, sort them by size and color, and graph the different results. Sort parts of a plant (stems, leaves, petals).

What You Should Be Seeing

You may find that the plant in the dark stays very moist. This is a great opportunity to talk in more depth about the sun. You might even talk about places around your house that would be good for growing plants due to the amount of sunlight they recieve.

Soil Erosion ❯

In this experiment, you and your child will demonstrate how erosion occurs and learn the value of keeping trees, plants, and grass living in our soil. Children will begin to understand the importance of having vegetation covering the soil.

 ## Talk Like Scientists!

- **Erosion**—the gradual destruction of something by natural forces (such as water, wind, or ice); the process by which something is worn away
- **Soil**—the upper layer of earth that may be dug or plowed and in which plants grow
- **Vegetation**—plant life or plant cover over a portion of Earth's surface

How to Do It

1. Begin a discussion with your child about erosion and vegetation. Ask, "What can you tell me about the word erosion?" "Why do we have grass, plants, and trees on Earth's surface?"
2. Record your child's thoughts on what causes erosion and research further if she is curious to see the effects of erosion on beaches or mountains. Continue to explore her ideas and questions throughout the activity.
3. To start, lay milk containers on their sides and cut out one side (to make an opening for soil) in the three containers.
4. Fill the containers with garden soil and press down firmly in the container. Put an extra inch of soil in bottle 1. In bottle 2 put an inch of mulch (wood chips, dead leaves, and sticks). In bottle 3 put a layer of grass (could be removed from overgrowth of your yard).
5. Place the three milk containers on a table where the neck of the bottle will overhang and place a bowl or container under each milk container to capture overflow water.
6. Slowly pour 1 cup of water on top of the soil and cover soil surface in each of the jugs.
7. Encourage your child's curiosity: How much water do you think we will capture in our collection cup for each milk container?
8. Encourage your child's critical-thinking skills: What can you tell me about the importance of ground cover on Earth's surface? What can you tell me about erosion?

Predict and Hypothesize

- Problem solve with your child: I wonder what will happen if we add water over the next one or two weeks to each container.
- Pour one cup of water every two days into each container and measure how much water is collected. Also note if anything is happening to the soil in the containers.
- Test the hypothesis by measuring water. Chart what you discover.

What You Should Be Seeing

If the soil level is above the neck of the bottle, you may see the materials clogging up the opening.

Add more STEAM activities:

Technology—Use a stopwatch to see how long it takes for water to be collected in a smaller container.
Engineering—Discuss, plan, and draw other types of containers to show soil cover and water collection.
Arts—Draw/paint landscapes with ground cover.
Math—Chart how much water is collected and note on a chart.

PART 2

TECHNOLOGY

What Is a Machine? ❯

Children will identify machines and begin to learn that they are technologies that have been invented.

 Talk Like Technology Experts!

- **Machine**—an instrument (such as a lever) designed to transmit or modify the application of power, force, or motion
- **Part**—one of the pieces that are put together to form a machine
- **Purpose**—the reason why something is done or used
- **Technology**—the use of science in industry, engineering, and so on to invent useful things or to solve problems
- **Tool**—a device, often handheld, that aids in accomplishing a task

How to Do It

1. Begin by asking your child, "What is a machine?" "What is technology?"
2. Talk about your child's ideas about machines. If he is curious, look up images or videos about tools, machines, and technology.
3. Gather many tools, equipment, and machines to look at from your home.
4. Look carefully at one machine at a time. Ask, "What does this machine do, and how does it make it easier to do work or play?"
5. Ask your child, "What materials were used to make the machine?" "How does it move?" "What makes it work?"
6. Ask him to look at the machines that have moving parts. Examples: hands on the clock move to tell time, the blades on a fan turn to circulate air.
7. Find a piece of equipment that can be taken apart. Make sure it is safe (remove electrical cords and look for sharp pieces). Discuss the parts as you take the machine apart.
8. Encourage your child's curiosity: Why do you think most machines have more than one part?
9. Encourage your child's critical-thinking skills: What can you tell me about machines?

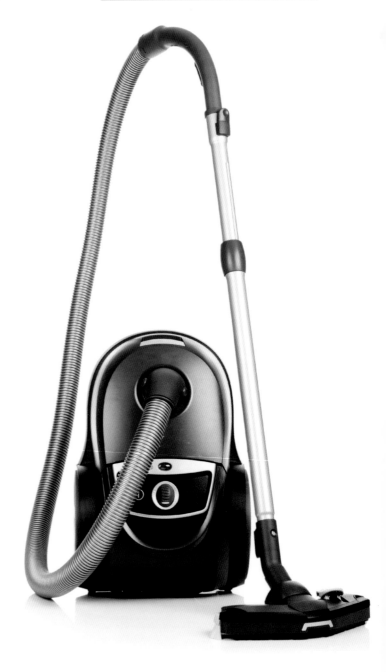

Predict and Hypothesize

- Problem solve with your child: I wonder if there are more machines in the kitchen or the rest of the house.
- Predict and hypothesize the answer to the question. Test the hypothesis and record what you discover.

Add more STEAM activities:

Science—Discuss physics of machines and review videos.

Engineering—Plan and create a new machine.

Arts—Make a drawing of machines. Draw or paint your favorite machine.

Math—Sort and categorize the machines.

Balance Scale—Exploring Weight❯

Children will use household items to make a balance scale to learn about heavier and lighter weights.

What You Need

- Plastic coat hanger with hooks or indentations on top
- Weights of some kind (bead, washer, bolt)
- String
- 2 baskets
- Digital scale (optional)
- STEAM journal

 Talk Like Technology Experts!

- **Balance scale**—an instrument or machine for weighing
- **Density**—the distribution of a quantity (as mass, electricity, or energy) per unit
- **Heavy**—having great weight in proportion to bulk
- **Light**—having relatively little weight in proportion to bulk
- **Mass**—the property of a body that is a measure of the amount of material it contains, that causes it to have weight
- **Weight**—a unit of weight or mass

How to Do It

1. Talk to your child about heavy and light objects around him and engage his curiosity by asking, "What would be heavier and weigh more—three books or three quarters?" Tell him that you will be making a balance scale to show which is heavier.
2. If your child is interested in learning more, look up images or videos about balance scales.
3. Use a plastic hanger that has hooks or indentations on the top.
4. Cut eight pieces of string the same length (approximately 12 to 15 inches).
5. Tie four strings to one basket and four strings to the other basket.
6. Secure onto the hanger and make sure each basket is the same distance from the hanger.
7. Hang your new balance scale and place items in each basket. If the baskets are the same weight and "balanced," the mass is the same. If one basket drops lower than the other basket, that basket has more weight (or mass).
8. Encourage your child's curiosity: Why do you think one basket is lower than the other basket?
9. Encourage your child's critical-thinking skills: What can you tell me about heavier and lighter weights?

Predict and Hypothesize

- Problem solve with your child: I wonder what will happen if we try different items from around our house.
- Predict and hypothesize the answer to the question. Test the hypothesis and record what you discover.

Add more STEAM activities:

Science—Discuss physics terms of mass and balance and encourage children to try to have their scale balance by adding items to one side or the other.

Engineering—Plan and create a balance scale that can weigh bigger items.

Arts—Make a drawing of things in the home and label each as either heavy or light.

Math—Sort and record the data of heavy and light OR actual weight if a digital scale is used.

Make a Solar Oven ❯

Children will make a solar oven to learn about the energy of the sun. You will also use the sun's heat to warm some nachos with cheese!

What You Need

- Pizza box (or similarly shaped box)
- Sheet of plastic
- Foil
- Tape
- Piece of wire
- Warm, sunny day
- STEAM journal

 Talk Like Technology Experts!

- **Oven**—a chamber used for baking, heating, or drying
- **Solar energy**—energy produced by or using the sun's light or heat

How to Do It

1. Discuss with your child how the heat of the sun can warm things, which is called solar energy. Ask, "What happens in our oven?" Ask him to imagine how people cooked before the oven was invented.
2. If needed, or if your child is curious to learn more, go online to find out more about solar ovens. Discuss his observations about solar energy throughout the activity.
3. Cut out almost the entire top of the lid of the pizza box. Cut on only three sides so that one side stays as a hinge to make a solar panel.
4. Tape a large piece of plastic to the underside of the lid. Make sure it is taped all around to make a good seal.
5. Line the bottom and sides inside the box with foil.
6. Cover the inside portion of the cut-out lid with foil, then use a small piece of wire to hold the panel open.
7. Put some nachos with a little bit of cheese sprinkled over the nachos inside the tin foil bottom.
8. Close the panel and place the oven in a sunny spot so that the solar panel faces direct sunlight.
9. Wait until you see the cheese start to melt, and then eat!
10. Encourage your child's curiosity: What would happen if we tried this experiment early in the morning with very little sun?
11. Encourage your child's critical-thinking skills: What can you tell me about a solar oven?

Predict and Hypothesize

- Problem solve with your child: I wonder what would happen if we tried other foods in our solar oven.
- Predict and hypothesize the answer to the question. Test the hypothesis and record what you discover.

Add more STEAM activities:

Science—Discuss solar energy and its importance as an alternative energy source. Talk about other things that use solar energy.

Engineering—Design and create a different type of solar oven.

Arts—Draw pictures of things that use solar energy.

Math—Record the outside temperature and time how long it takes the cheese to melt at 9:00 a.m., 12 noon, 2:00 p.m., and 4:00 p.m.

Did You Know?

- Solar panels—the most common form of solar energy used today—absorb the sun's light to heat water or create electricity.
- Solar energy is one of the cleanest and most abundant renewable energy sources available.

Build a Potato-Powered Lightbulb ❯

Children will build a potato-powered lightbulb to learn about electrical currents and energy.

Talk Like Technology Experts!

- **Battery**—a device that is placed inside a machine (such as a clock, toy, or car) to supply it with electricity
- **Chemical reaction**—a change that occurs when two or more substances combine to form a new substance
- **Circuit**—the complete path of an electric current
- **Electrical current**—a flow of electric charge
- **Electrical energy**—usable energy from electricity
- **Resistance**—the opposition offered by a body or substance to the passage through it of a steady electric current

What You Need

- 3 potatoes
- 3 copper pennies (pennies made between 1962 to 1982 are 95 percent copper)
- 4 pieces of copper wire (approximately 3 to 4 inches—#12 or #18) with insulation removed from each end
- 3 galvanized nails
- 3 crocodile clips
- Knife or wire pliers (adult use only)
- Scissors
- LED (small, low-current LEDs that need only 1 or 2 mA (milliamperes) to run)
- Voltmeter/multimeter (optional)
- STEAM journal

How to Do It

1. Support your child's understanding by asking, "What happens with a toy when we put a battery into it?" Talk with him about how you can make energy using a potato. Discuss how, prior to modern electrification, people did not have any electricity in their homes to power lights, stoves, refrigerators, air conditioners, and so on. Listen to his ideas and conduct further research online or at your library if he is curious to learn more about electricity.

2. Cut a small slit into one end of each potato for insertion of the coin. Insert a copper penny into one end of each potato and insert a nail into the other end.

3. Take each piece of wire and remove the plastic insulation from both ends, exposing around three centimeters (1.18 inches) of the copper wire. A knife or wire pliers can be used (adult use).

4. Wrap one end of the wire around the top of a crocodile clip. Make sure good contact is made between the exposed copper from the wire and the metal clip. Clip the crocodile clip onto the coin wedged into the potato. Repeat this process for three of the wires.

5. Wrap the exposed copper ends (on "loose" end of crocodile clip) around the nail of the "neighboring" potato. Do this two times.

6. Take the fourth wire and wrap one end around the last free nail.

7. You should have the following sequence: first potato (loose copper wire and nail wired to crocodile clip on second potato); second potato (nail wired to crocodile clip from first potato and from nail to crocodile clip on third potato); and third potato (nail wired to crocodile clip from second potato and from nail with loose wire).

8. Your potato battery is now set up. The coin is the positive part and your nail is the negative part of your battery. If you have a multimeter, you can check the battery by making contact with the free wires (coin to red probe and nail to black probe).

9. To light up your LED, wrap the free wire at the coin end around the long end of the LED, and wrap the free wire from the nail around the short end of the LED. Do not let the two copper wires touch each other directly.

10. You can connect more potatoes for more power if you have the materials.

11. Encourage your child's curiosity: What would happen if we added more potatoes?

12. Encourage your child's critical-thinking skills: What can you tell me about making a battery out of potatoes?

Predict and Hypothesize

- Problem solve with your child: I wonder what would happen if we tried using lemons instead of potatoes.
- Predict and hypothesize the answer to the question. Test the hypothesis and record what you discover.

Add more STEAM activities:

Science—Discuss chemical reactions and how scientists and engineers are important to finding out about other energy sources. You may also want to experiment with other food sources (bananas, tomatoes).

Engineering—Design and create other types of batteries.

Arts—Draw pictures of your battery.

Math—Record the amperage you get from different numbers of potatoes (or other battery sources).

What You Should Be Seeing

For this experiment to work, a continuous circuit or connection must be made between the potatoes and connections. You may see only a small amount of electric current. One problem to look for might be that your potato is not moist enough to conduct the electricity.

Make a Sundial ❯

Children will build a sundial to learn how to tell time by the sun's position in the sky.

 Talk Like Technology Experts!

- **Clock**—a device for indicating or measuring time, commonly by means of hands moving on a dial
- **Sundial**—a device that is used to show the time of day by the position of the sun and that consists of a plate with markings like a clock and an object with a straight edge that casts a shadow onto the plate
- **Time**—a point of time measured as seconds, minutes, hours, days, years, and so on

What You Need
- Paper plate
- Pen or pencil
- Marker
- Clock
- Sunny day and area with plenty of sun
- STEAM journal

How to Do It

1. Engage your child's curiosity by asking, "What is time?" You can ask her further questions to help guide her learning, such as "What time do you usually go to bed?" "What time do you get up in the morning?" "How do you know what time it is?" Discuss the importance of time and how the technology of the sundial has helped people throughout history.
2. Make a small hole in the center of the plate and insert one end of the pencil (or pen) so that the pencil is standing straight up.
3. Place the plate, with pencil inserted, in an outdoor spot free from shade. You may need to secure it so that the wind will not blow it away or move it in any way.
4. Every hour on the hour use the marker to draw the shadow of the pencil and write down the time.
5. Do this for all the daylight hours.
6. Encourage your child's curiosity: What happens to our sundial at night?
7. Encourage your child's critical-thinking skills: What can you tell me about making a sundial to tell time?

Predict and Hypothesize

- Problem solve with your child: I wonder what would happen if we tried the experiment on a night with a full moon.
- Predict and hypothesize the answer to the question. Test the hypothesis and record what you discover.

Add more STEAM activities:

Science—Discuss the importance of time for all parts of our life and how animals also use schedules even though they do not tell time.

Engineering—Design and create other types of sundials.

Arts—Draw pictures of ancient sundials.

Math—Measure the distance between each line to see if they are the same (or close) distance apart.

Did You Know?

Around 280 BC, Aristarchus of Samos was credited with the invention of the hemispherical sundial, or hemicycle, which consisted of a block of stone or wood that had a hemisphere-shaped groove cut into it. A pointer was placed on one end of the groove. The path that the shadow followed was more or less a circular arc.

Using Coding

Children will learn about computer coding by completing a challenge course with obstacles.

 Talk Like Technology Experts!

- **Binary code**—relating to or involving a method of calculating and of representing information, especially in computers by using the numbers 0 and 1
- **Coding**—instructions for a computer
- **Computer**—a programmable, usually electronic, device that can store, retrieve, and process data
- **Computer program**—a sequence of coded instructions that can be inserted into a computer
- **Computer programmer**—a person who prepares and tests programs for computers
- **Technology**—the use of science in industry, engineering, and so on, to invent useful things or to solve problems

What You Need

- Index cards, sheets of paper, or paper plates
- Obstacles (items that can "block" or interfere with walking forward, such as chairs, tables, toys, cones, balls)
- STEAM journal

How to Do It

1. Prepare to collaborate on the challenge by asking, "What is a computer?" Discuss computers, coding, and the importance of coding/computer programming in technology. You are building a foundation for children to solve problems and start to think like a computer programmer.
2. There are many wonderful resources available online, so if your child is interested in learning more, search for videos about coding for children.
3. Create a series of cards called arrow cards. These cards can be constructed from everyday items including index cards, sheets of paper, or paper plates. In total, you will create eight cards for each category: forward, right, and left. In addition, you will create a "start" card and a "finish" card.
4. Determine the start and finish point and put the start and finish cards in place in a room.
5. Put obstacles in the area between the start and finish card route.
6. For the first game, the adult should be the "programmer" and give instructions, and the child can be the "computer" and follow the instructions.
7. Example: The "computer" takes three steps forward (obstacle), turns right and takes three steps, turns left and takes two steps, turns right and takes two steps, then finishes right in front of you, the "programmer."
8. You may want to draw it out on a grid to show him how it worked. You might ask if there were other ways he may have gone to get to the finish and still avoid the obstacles.
9. Allow your child to be the programmer and give you instructions to get to the finish.
10. As the game progresses (and on a different day), you could preplan and put out the direction cards before starting the game.
11. Explain that if the programmer does not give good directions, the computer will not be able to get to the finish.
12. Encourage your child's curiosity: What do you need to do or plan for an obstacle?
13. Encourage your child's critical-thinking skills: What can you tell me about being the programmer and giving me instructions?

Predict and Hypothesize

- Problem solve with your child: I wonder if you could listen to the directions and find the finish with your eyes covered.
- Predict and hypothesize the answer to the question. Test the hypothesis and record what you discover.

Add more STEAM activities:

Science—Discuss how patterns are found in nature and science and how computers need and use patterns for coding. There are many free coding apps and coding toys available.

Engineering—Design and create other symbols for your challenge course.

Arts—Make a coding bracelet or necklace of your name.

Math—Make a grid and/or schematic for the game.

Did You Know?

Some tasks that are controlled through computer coding include:

- Hot water heaters
- Traffic lights
- Elevators

Make a Coloring Robot ❯

Children will build a robot that draws in order to learn about robots in technology and how robots can be used in our world.

Talk Like Technology Experts!

- **Battery**—a device that is placed inside a machine (such as a clock, toy, or car) to supply it with electricity
- **Motor**—a rotating machine that transforms electrical energy into mechanical energy
- **Robot**—a machine that can do the work of a person and that works automatically or is controlled by a computer

What You Need

- Plastic cup
- Electrical tape
- 3–4 markers (different colors)
- 1.5–3 V DC motor (from electronics store or old toy)
- 2 AAA battery holder (from electronics store)
- 2 AAA batteries
- Items to make device off-balance (clothespin, wooden craft stick, and so on)
- Optional decorations (markers for face, and so on)
- STEAM journal

How to Do It

1. Begin by asking your child, "What is a robot?" Discuss how robots have been created to help industries and businesses.
2. Listen to your child's ideas and talk about them. If your child is curious to learn more, look up images or videos geared toward children about making robots.
3. Use electrical tape to attach the markers into the cup as legs. You can use three, but using more with different colors will enhance the art designs.
4. Wrap the wire around the leads on the motor to attach the battery pack to the DC motor. ⚠ **Safety Note: Only adults should handle batteries.**
5. Tape the DC motor on top of the cup.
6. Tape the battery pack on top of the cup next to the DC motor. Make sure it is all a little off center.
7. Place the batteries into the holder and watch the device vibrate. You can add weight onto one side of the top to make the device wiggle more.
8. When you are ready for your device to draw, remove caps of markers, place it in the center of the paper, and insert batteries.

9. Encourage your child's curiosity: What happens as we change the amount of weight on our robot?

10. Encourage your child's critical-thinking skills: What can you tell me about making a robot that draws?

Predict and Hypothesize
- Problem solve with your child: I wonder what would happen if we added more legs.
- Predict and hypothesize the answer to the question. Test the hypothesis and record what you discover.

Add more STEAM activities:
Science—Discuss how robotics are being used in science and manufacturing.
Engineering—Design and create other robots.
Arts—Decorate your robot.
Math—Analyze whether the robot makes any patterns.

What You Should be Seeing
Basically, this first "robot" is just a cup with colored markers for legs that vibrates and spins due to the motor being off-balance. As it vibrates around on a piece of paper it makes designs. The coloring robot is not an example of a modern-day robot since it is not programmable and has no controller.

Smartphone Projector
Children will build a projector with a magnifying glass, box, and smartphone to explore image magnification and projection.

 ## Talk Like Technology Experts!

What You Need
- Small cardboard box
- Magnifying glass or camera lens
- Scissors, X-ACTO knife, or small serrated knife (adult use only)
- Tape
- Smartphone
- STEAM journal

- **Magnifying glass**—a specially shaped piece of glass that is attached to a handle and is used to make an object look larger than it is
- **Projector**—an optical instrument for projecting an image upon a surface
- **Smartphone**—a cell phone that includes additional software functions such as email or an Internet browser

How to Do It
1. Spark curiosity by asking your child, "What is a projector?" Talk about visiting the movie theater and how a projector is used to make a big picture on the screen. Discuss how the first projectors were used in movie houses. You may want to research this subject online to find more information to share with your child.

2. Trace the size of the magnifying glass on the front of a box, then cut the circle into the box. The circle should be a little smaller than the traced circle.

3. Tape the magnifying glass to the inside of the box so the lens matches up with the opening.

4. Use the circle from the cardboard or any other cardboard you have to make a stand for the smartphone. Position the smartphone so that it will project out of the magnifying glass. You may need to lock the phone into landscape position. Whatever is on your smartphone screen will be projected (photo, video, and so on.) You may need to connect the smartphone to a speaker to increase volume.

5. Point the projector to a white (or light) wall. Focus the picture by moving the phone toward or away from the lens. Close the box once it is focused. It helps to have the room fairly dark.

6. Encourage your child's curiosity: What happens as we move the box closer to the wall?

7. Encourage your child's critical-thinking skills: What can you tell me about making a projector?

Predict and Hypothesize

- Problem solve with your child: I wonder what would happen if we used different magnifying glasses.
- Predict and hypothesize the answers to the questions. Test the hypothesis and record what you discover.

Add more STEAM activities:

Science—Discuss how the lens is convex, which produces magnification.

Engineering—Design and create other projectors.

Arts—Decorate your projector.

Math—Measure the distance of the projector from the wall and how things change as you move the projector closer or farther.

Did You Know?

- A movie projector is an optomechanical (opto means optical) device for displaying motion picture film by projecting it onto a screen.
- An early movie projector, the zoopraxiscope, was invented by British photographer Eadweard Muybridge in 1879. The zoopraxiscope projected images from rotating glass disks in quick succession to give the viewer an impression of motion.

Making a Magnetic-Powered Car ❯

Children will build a magnetic-powered car to gain an understanding of magnetism and force.

 Talk Like Technology Experts!

- **Force**—strength or energy exerted or brought to bear
- **Magnet**—a piece of material (such as iron or steel) that is able to attract certain metals
- **Magnetism**—the property of attracting certain metals
- **Mass**—the property of a body that is a measurement of the amount of material that it contains, that causes it to have weight

What You Need

- Toy car
- Road tape (available at craft stores) or painter's tape
- 2 magnets, if possible one should be a bar magnet
  ⚠ Safety Note:
  Keep a close eye on small children when using loose parts such as magnets. Magnets are a choking hazard for young children, so supervision is critical.
- STEAM journal

How to Do It

1. Begin the activity by asking your child, "What is a magnet?" Discuss how alternative means of power are being explored for use in our cars.
2. Talk with your child about what you notice about magnets and conduct further research if he is curious to see more types of magnets.
3. Tape a magnet to the top of the toy car. Test your toy car by using a second magnet to "push" or "pull" it by moving it toward the toy car.
4. Lay down a road for your magnetic-powered car. This is not necessary to test your car but it does make it more fun.
5. You can experiment by using a ring, horseshoe, or other magnets.
6. Experiment to see if you can make the cars turn, go up a hill, or go backward.
7. Encourage your child's curiosity: What would happen if we used different magnets?
8. Encourage your child's critical-thinking skills: What can you tell me about making a magnetic-powered car?

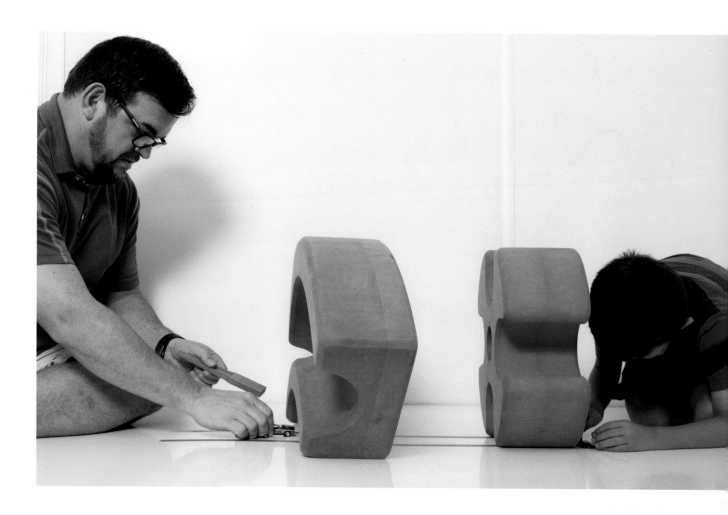

Predict and Hypothesize

- Problem solve with your child: I wonder what would happen if we used different cars with different weights.
- Predict and hypothesize the answer to the question. Test the hypothesis and record what you discover.

Did You Know?

Magnets are used for many purposes in everyday life, including:

- Making a tight seal on the doors to refrigerators and freezers
- Powering speakers in stereos and earphones
- Scanning machines that doctors use to look inside people's bodies, called MRIs (magnetic resonance imagers)

Add more STEAM activities:

Science—Discuss how you can push or pull the car without touching it.

Engineering—Use blocks and boxes to create a city for your roads.

Arts—Decorate your city.

Math—Switch the magnets and record responses. See how far they "push" your car.

Build a Robotic Hand ❯

In this engineering activity, children will build a robotic hand to discover more about the growing field of robotics.

 Talk Like Technology Experts!

- **Robot**—a machine that can do the work of a person and that works automatically or is controlled by a computer
- **Robotic technology**—machinery and equipment that is used to design, build, and operate robots

What You Need
- Tape
- Scissors
- Pencil
- Cardboard paper or cardstock paper
- Standard drinking straws
- Larger diameter straws (smoothie straws)
- Yarn or twine (will need different colored yarn)
- Optional—larger plastic needle
- STEAM journal

How to Do It

1. Engage your child by asking, "What is a robot?" "What do you think is meant by a robotic hand?" Discuss how advancements in robotics are changing people's lives.
2. To learn more about robotics, look up images or videos about robots or that show a robotic hand being built.
3. Trace the "robotic" hand on cardboard or cardstock. It may be useful to use a large adult hand first or cut the hand a little bigger than the actual tracing. You can try tracing the child's hand later.
4. Mark the finger joints on the cutout and fold the cutout on those lines like the natural bend in the hand at the finger, knuckle, and fingertip.
5. Cut smaller straws to the size of those three pieces (leave a little gap in between for movement).
6. Tape three straw pieces to each finger, one between each joint, for a total of fifteen straw pieces.
7. Tape a longer straw piece on the palm, leading from each finger to the wrist.
8. Each finger will have a length of yarn of its own. Make sure to secure the beginning of the thread on top of the finger. Thread each yarn through the three straws on the finger, then one straw on the palm. Leave about 10 inches of yarn.
9. Tape a larger straw on the wrist area, then thread all five pieces of yarn through the larger straw.
10. Experiment with "pulling" different pieces of yarn to see how to move the fingers on the robotic hand.
11. Encourage your child's curiosity: What happens if we pull two pieces of yarn at the same time?
12. Encourage your child's critical-thinking skills: What can you tell me about making a robotic hand?

Predict and Hypothesize

- Problem solve with your child: I wonder what would happen if we made a smaller hand.
- Predict and hypothesize the answer to the question. Test the hypothesis and record what you discover.

Add more STEAM activities:

Science—Show how your robotic hand is similar to muscles, ligaments, and tendons in a real hand. Discuss how a robotic hand might be used for those individuals who do not have functioning hands.

Engineering—Try different materials to build a robotic hand. Can you extend up into the arm?

Arts—Draw or decorate your robotic hand.

Math—Measure how far you would pull the yarn to make the fingers bend.

Build a Balloon-Powered Train Engine ❯

Children will build a balloon-powered train engine to learn how an engine makes things move.

Talk Like Technology Experts!

- **Engine**—a machine for converting any of various forms of energy into mechanical force and motion
- **Steam engine**—an engine driven or powered by steam

What You Need

- Paper towel tube
- Egg carton
- 2 straws
- 2 small rubber bands and 1 large rubber band
- 4 bottle caps for wheels
- Glue gun
- Balloon
- Leaf or flower
- Tape (optional)
- Hole punch (optional)
- STEAM journal

How to Do It

1. Begin by asking your child, "What does a train do?" Talk about how the steam engine is a type of technology that was first built over three hundred years ago. Discuss the importance of steam engines and trains throughout history and in our lives today.
2. If needed, or if your child is curious to view them, you may want to look up images of steam engines and trains to spark further questions and conversation.
3. Discuss how you will use air to power your engine instead of steam. Hold a leaf or flower in front of you and blow on it. Talk with your child about what happens to the leaf or flower when you blow on it.
4. Build the base of the engine by attaching the wheels (glued-on bottle caps) to the axle (straws). Secure the straws by using rubber bands. You might also secure the straws by using a hole punch and placing the straws through the holes prior to gluing the wheels in place.
5. Glue the long tube on top of the egg carton.
6. Glue the short tube on top of the long tube.
7. Blow up a balloon and secure it with a larger rubber band before releasing the air out of the balloon. Once everything is in place, allow air to be released from the balloon. It is the release of

air that will "power" or "move" the train forward. You may need to use tape to secure the rubber band to the balloon.

8. Encourage your child's curiosity: What happens if we blow up the balloon only a little?
9. Encourage your child's critical-thinking skills: What can you tell me about making a balloon-powered engine?

Predict and Hypothesize

- Problem solve with your child: I wonder what would happen if we used different sizes of balloons.
- Predict and hypothesize the answer to the question. Test the hypothesis and record what you discover.

Add more STEAM activities:

Science—Discuss how steam was used for steam engines. You may also attach one magnet to the front of the train and use a handheld magnet to move the train.

Engineering—Try using different materials to build your train.

Arts—Decorate your train. Sing songs about trains.

Math—Measure how far your train goes with different sizes of balloons.

Did You Know?

- A steam engine is able to harness the energy of steam to move machinery. Steam engines were used to great effect to run locomotives and steamships. They are still used today to help run nuclear power plants.
- Early in the first century AD, a Greek inventor named Heron of Alexandria designed the world's first aeolipile, an early steam turbine.

Build an Abacus ❯

An abacus is the first known constructed calculator. Children will build an abacus to gain an understanding of early technology and basic math.

What You Need

- Medium-sized box
- String
- Small colored beads (30–50)
- Pencil
- Ruler
- Nail
- STEAM journal

Talk Like Technology Experts!

- **Abacus**—an instrument for performing mathematical calculations by sliding counters along rods or in grooves
- **Calculator**—a usually electronic device for performing mathematical calculations

How to Do It

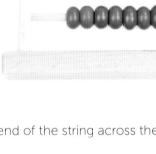

1. Start a discussion with your child by asking, "What can we use to count or add things together?" Children may mention counting on their fingers or they may be familiar with a calculator. Talk about how an abacus was invented many years ago to help people count.
2. While looking at an image or video of an abacus, talk with your child about what you notice. Continue to communicate and ask questions throughout the activity.
3. Mark off three to five even spaces along one side of a medium box and about ½ inch (1.27 centimeters) down from the top. Do the same on the opposite side of the box.
4. Use a nail to make small holes at each mark.
5. Pull one end of string through the first hole and tie a knot securely on the outside of the box.
6. String ten colored beads on the string and fasten the other end of the string across the box to the other side.
7. Do the same with the other pieces of string. **Tip: Try to limit the abacus to three to five rows.**
8. Find things you can count. Examples include trees in the yard, how many times your child can hop on one foot, number of carrots on his plate, and so on.
9. Encourage your child's curiosity: What happens if we run out of beads on one row?
10. Encourage your child's critical-thinking skills: What can you tell me about using an abacus?

Predict and Hypothesize

- Problem solve with your child: I wonder if there is anything we could count so that we run out of beads.
- Predict and hypothesize the answer to the question. Test the hypothesis and record what you discover.

Add more STEAM activities:

Science—Use the abacus to count flowers, insects, and what you find in nature.

Engineering—Try using different materials to build your abacus.

Arts—Decorate your abacus.

Math—Record and chart measurements on different items.

Did You Know?

The abacus is a calculating tool that was in use in China, Europe, and Russia centuries before a written numeral system. The exact origin of the abacus is unknown; although, it may have been a Babylonian invention. Today, abaci are often made with bamboo and beads sliding on wires, but originally they were made from beans or stones. The abacus remains in common use in some parts of the world.

PART 3

ENGINEERING

Building Using Recycled Materials 〉

Children will build using recycled materials to learn about basic engineering concepts and the possibilities of reuse for everyday items.

 Talk Like Engineers!

- **Construct**—to build or make something physical, such as a road, bridge, or building
- **Engineer**—a person who has scientific training and who designs and builds complicated products, machines, systems, or structures
- **Recycle**— to use again or to remake an item into something new
- **Waste**—items thrown away, often called trash or garbage

What You Need

- All sorts of recyclable materials—plastic containers (margarine, milk, yogurt, produce), boxes (cereal, tissue, jewelry, storage), parts from old toys, cleaned-out cans, egg crates, paper, paper towel rolls, string, old shoelaces, paper or plastic plates, bowls, cups, and so on
- Tape
- Scissors
- STEAM journal

How to Do It

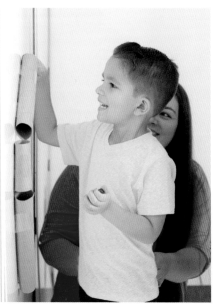

1. Begin a conversation by asking your child, "I've gathered a lot of materials I could throw out. What do you think you could build with some of it?" Talk about the work of an engineer, someone who designs and builds things. You may need to start out by asking some questions. "Can you build a house, road, or bridge?"
2. You may want to look up images or videos about engineers and construction, or about products made from recycled materials.
3. Discuss and plan what should be built first using the recycled materials you gathered. Invite your child to create the structure.
4. Ask what she wants to build next and what materials she plans to use.
5. Urge your child to experiment and try different materials.
6. Encourage your child to add their own toys and create a little city.
7. Encourage your child's curiosity: What types of materials do you think will work best to create your building?
8. Encourage your child's critical-thinking skills: What can you tell me about building with recycled materials?

Predict and Hypothesize

- Problem solve with your child: I wonder what will happen if we use only one type of material to build a structure.
- Predict and hypothesize the answer to the question. Test the hypothesis and record what you discover.

Add more STEAM activities:

Science—Discuss the importance of recycling to protect our environment.
Technology—Take pictures of various parts of the structures.
Arts—Dramatic play is important! Encourage your child to make up a story and use her toys in her city.
Math—Sort and chart the different types of materials that were used.

Using Blueprints ❯

Children will build with blocks, using blueprints to further their learning about the fundamentals of construction and engineering concepts.

What You Need

- Large piece of paper
- Paper shapes the same size and shapes of the blocks to be used
- Blocks (variety of shapes)
- STEAM journal

 ## Talk Like Engineers!

- **Blueprint**—a photographic print that shows how something (such as a building) will be made
- **Construct**—to build or make something physical, such as a road, bridge, or building
- **Engineer**—a person who has scientific training and who designs and builds complicated products, machines, systems, or structures

How to Do It

1. Make your own blueprint for your child to see. Ask what she can tell you about the design. Talk about the job of an engineer, someone who builds and designs things. You may need to start out by asking some questions, such as "How many blocks would this design take?" "How many different shapes are included?" Also discuss how many things are built using a blueprint or a design. Continue to discuss the role of engineers and the importance of blueprints in their work.

2. Let your child first try to follow your blueprint design. Initially, you may want to make it a puzzle by laying the pieces randomly over the design sheet.
3. Next, encourage your child to make different blueprints and follow up by building that design.
4. If a design does not balance, you can discuss why.
5. Encourage your child's curiosity: What types of shapes work best for the bottom of your structure?
6. Encourage your child's critical-thinking skills: What can you tell me about building using a blueprint?

Predict and Hypothesize

- Problem solve with your child: I wonder how tall we can make a structure before it falls.
- Predict and hypothesize the answer to the question. Test the hypothesis and record what you discover.

Add more STEAM activities:

Science—Encourage your child to build a bridge to take a car over a river. This will help her understand the need for a base of support.

Technology—Take pictures of the different blueprints so your child can come back and use them later to build.

Arts—Use different colors of paper and discuss patterns.

Math—Sort and chart the different shapes used in the structures.

Pompom Tunnel Highway 〉

Children will build a "highway" of tunnels to show how gravity will roll their pompoms to the floor.

 Talk Like Engineers!

- **Construct**—to build or make something physical, such as a road, bridge, or building
- **Engineer**—a person who has scientific training and who designs and builds complicated products, machines, systems, or structures
- **Gravity**—the force that causes things to fall toward Earth
- **Tunnel**—a protected or covered passageway

What You Need

- Small pompoms (marbles, Ping-Pong balls, small toys)
- Cylinders (paper towel rolls, wrapping paper rolls, plastic cups)
- Tape
- Open wall area
- STEAM journal

How to Do It

1. Talk about how gravity pulls things down to the ground. Ask, "When I throw this pompom up in the air—what happens?"
2. Listen to your child's ideas and talk about them. Continue to discuss your child's ideas about gravity.
3. Start by taping one "tunnel," one of the cylinders, up on the wall. Test by dropping the pompom through the tunnel to make sure it will fit and fall to the floor.
4. Plan where to place the next tunnel, but before taping it to the wall, try dropping it to see that it goes into the second tunnel and that the space in between works to keep the pompom moving.
5. Continue the experiment by adding additional tunnels. You may want to start a second series of tunnels that have less angle and/or more changes of direction.
6. Encourage your child's curiosity: Does the pompom move faster in a tunnel that faces more to the floor/ground?
7. Encourage your child's critical-thinking skills: What can you tell me about gravity that you learned from our tunnel highway?

Predict and Hypothesize

- Problem solve with your child: I wonder what would happen if we used other items in our tunnel highway (small rocks, Ping-Pong ball, marble, small toy).
- Predict and hypothesize the answer to the question. Test the hypothesis and record what you discover.

Add more STEAM activities:

Science—Discuss and experiment with how different weighted objects react to gravity.

Technology—Take pictures or videos of your tunnel highway.

Arts—Decorate the different tunnels.

Math—Time how long it takes different substances to go through the tunnel.

Did You Know?

- A *blueprint* is a reproduction of a technical drawing, documenting an architectural or an engineering design.
- Blueprints became blue in the 1840s when the cyanotype process was invented by John Herschel. It was intended as a means of reproducing notes and drawings but was adopted by scientists and others interested in photography.

Straw Rocket ❯

Children will make rockets that they can "launch" by blowing into a straw. This activity will introduce the concepts of propulsion and force.

 ### Talk Like Engineers!

- **Air resistance**—a pushing force that slows things down
- **Force**—a push or pull on an object; in this case, how hard you blow or push air through the straw
- **Gravity**—a force that pulls things toward Earth
- **Launch**—to send or shoot something, such as a rocket, into the air, water, or outer space
- **Propel**—to drive forward or onward by means of a force
- **Rocket**—a cylindrical projectile that can be propelled to a great height or distance by the combustion of its contents

What You Need

- Straws—regular and smoothie size (with larger diameter)
- Tape or glue
- Markers or crayons
- Scissors
- Paper
- STEAM journal

How to Do It

1. Talk about how you will be making a simple paper rocket. Ask your child what she knows about rockets. Talk to your child about how aerospace engineers design, build, and launch rockets. You may want to look up videos about rockets and aerospace engineers to learn more.
2. Draw a picture of a rocket for your child.
3. Invite your child to color the rocket and cut it out.
4. Using the larger straw, tape or seal one end so it's completely sealed.
5. Cut the paper straw to fit the length of the rocket and attach it to the rocket with tape or glue with the sealed end at the top of the rocket.
6. Slide the smaller straw into the larger straw.
7. Point the straw up and blow into the straw to see the rocket take off.
8. Encourage your child's curiosity: Why do you think the rocket falls back to the ground after being launched in the air?
9. Encourage your child's critical-thinking skills: What can you tell me about launching a rocket?

Predict and Hypothesize

- Problem solve with your child: I wonder what would happen if we flew a bigger or smaller rocket.
- Predict and hypothesize the answer to the question. Test the hypothesis and record what you discover.

Add more STEAM activities:

Science—Discuss physics terms of mass, air resistance, and force. Try different angles and designs.

Technology—Try some of the more advanced rocket kits.

Arts—Make a drawing of the launch and landing of your rocket.

Math—Use a stopwatch and measure how long the rocket is in the air from launch to landing. Try several different trials and put them on a line graph.

Did You Know?

American rocketry pioneer Dr. Robert H. Goddard tested his first liquid-fueled rocket in 1926. Goddard is considered the father of modern rocket propulsion.

- The first rocket that could fly high enough to reach space was Germany's V2 missile, launched in 1942. The first rocket that launched something into space was used to launch Sputnik, the first satellite, in 1957.

Build a Zip Line ❯

Children will build a zip line from a high level to a low level to gain an understanding of inclined planes as well as the concepts of friction and gravity.

What You Need

- String/rope
- Scissors
- A high and low area to attach string/rope
- Carabiner
- Empty paint bucket
- Weighted items (rock, toy)
- STEAM journal

 Talk Like Engineers!

- **Construct**—build or erect something (typically a building, road, or machine)
- **Engineer**—a person who designs or builds a machine or structure
- **Friction**—the resistance of motion when one object rubs against the other; in this case, the resistance of carabiner or bucket handle rubbing against the rope
- **Gravity**—a force that pulls things toward Earth; in this case, it causes the car to go down the ramp
- **Inclined plane**—a sloping ramp that makes it easier to move things up or down; in this case, an angled zip line
- **Load**—the weight of an object

How to Do It

1. Show your child a picture of a zip line if she has never seen one. Discuss how gravity pulls anything on a zip line from a high level to a low level.
2. Collaborate with your child to build a zip line with a bucket that can transport materials from a high point to a low point. Tie your rope to an object at a high level. Tie a big knot or tie a small tree branch on the rope at a high level to "hold" your container or keep it from sliding down the rope.
3. Place the carabiner or bucket handle through the rope.
4. Tie off your rope at an angle and at a low level.
5. Try putting a rock into the bucket and releasing it down the zip line.
6. Encourage your child's curiosity: Does the heavier rock move faster or slower than a lighter rock?
7. Encourage your child's critical-thinking skills: What can you tell me about gravity and your zip line?

Predict and Hypothesize

- Problem solve with your child: I wonder what would happen if we used other items in the bucket to go down the zip line.
- Predict and hypothesize the answer to the question. Test the hypothesis and record what you discover.

Add more STEAM activities:

Science—Discuss and experiment with how different weighted objects react to gravity.

Technology—Take pictures or videos of your zip line.

Arts—Draw pictures and different designs for your zip line.

Math—Time how long it takes different objects to get to the ground (different weighted objects or a different angle).

Simple Machines (Lever) —Make a Launcher »

Explore mechanical terminology and learning by building a launcher with your child.

 ## Talk Like Engineers!

- **Force**—push or pull on an object; in this case, how hard you step or jump on the board
- **Gravity**—a force that pulls things toward Earth
- **Launch**—to propel something with force; to send or shoot something
- **Lever**—a stiff bar that rests on a support (fulcrum) to lift or move loads (for example, crowbar, wheelbarrow, oar)
- **Propel**—to drive forward or onward by means of a force

What You Need

- Wood, 24 to 32 inches long (this might be a yardstick, or 1" x 3" or 1" x 4" pine board)
- Something round to be used as a fulcrum (can, toy block, PVC pipe, large wooden dowel, log)
- Something to be launched (foam, beanbag, small ball, balled-up paper, balled-up plastic bag)
- May need to glue/screw on a container to hold object to be thrown or glue on some sandpaper
- An open space
- STEAM journal

How to Do It

1. Ask your child, "What can you tell me about launching (throwing) something up in the air?" Tell her you will be making a homemade launcher. Talk with your child about the lever, a simple machine.
2. Find or purchase a board or other appropriate launching board. (You may need to cut the board. To be safe, sand the corners so they are not sharp and sand the board if it is not smooth.)
3. Find something to act as the fulcrum (the longer the board, the larger the diameter needed for the fulcrum). Some suggest screwing the fulcrum into the board, but if you do that you will not be able to change the location easily, which will reduce the amount of exploration.
4. Prepare the area that will be used to launch the object. You may need to screw on a container or attach some sandpaper so the object will not slide.
5. Place the object to be launched into the launch area.
6. Step with some force onto the opposite end of the board and watch the object to be launched.
   ⚠ Safety Note: Be careful to keep your child's head and face clear of the launch.

7. You may encourage your child to run after the object to retrieve it or to catch it!
8. Explore moving the fulcrum location, adding more/less force, and changing out the item to be launched.
9. Encourage your child's curiosity: Why do you think some things go farther than other things?
10. Encourage your child's critical-thinking skills: What can you tell me about a homemade launcher?

Predict and Hypothesize

- Problem solve with your child: I wonder what will happen if we launch the same object but move the rounded piece (fulcrum).
- Predict and hypothesize the answer to the question. Test the hypothesis and record what you discover.

Add more STEAM activities:

Science—Discuss physics terms of mass, air resistance, and force. Try different weights and force and try moving the fulcrum.

Technology—Record your launches on video.

Arts—Make your own beanbags.

Math—Record the weight of items and compare to how far they are launched in distance.

Did You Know?

- The first simple machine was probably a strong stick (the lever) that our ancestors used to move a heavy object. The earliest writings regarding levers date from the third century BC.
- Popular levers used today include the seesaw, can opener, hammer, pliers, crowbar, wheelbarrow, oar, broom, tweezers, and many more!

Simple Machines (Wheel and Axle)—Make a Wind-Powered Car ❯

Together, you and your child will create a rolling car that can be powered by wind! This activity highlights the design constructs of the wheel and axle plus the power of the wind to make things go.

⚙ Talk Like Engineers!

- **Air resistance**—a pushing force that slows things down
- **Friction**—the resistance of motion when one object rubs against the other; in this case, the resistance of the car wheels moving over the surface
- **Wheel and axle**—a simple lifting machine consisting of a rope that unwinds from a wheel onto a cylindrical drum or shaft joined to the wheel to provide mechanical advantage
- **Wind**—a natural movement of air of any velocity
- **Wind energy**—the use of air flow through wind turbines to power generators for electric power; wind energy is one of the fastest growing forms of renewable energy

What You Need

- Materials to make body of the car (paper towel tube or cardboard box)
- Materials to make wheels (bottle caps, jar lids, cardboard circles, toy wheels)
- Materials to make axle (skewers, straws)
- Materials to secure "sail" (skewers, stick, wooden craft stick)
- Materials to make "sail" (cardstock, construction paper, plastic)
- Something to generate air (fan, outside wind, blowing air through a straw)
- Hole punch
- Tape
- Scissors
- Playdough (optional)
- Stopwatch and measuring tape (optional)
- STEAM journal

How to Do It

1. Ask your child, "What can you tell me about wheels?" It may be helpful to point out some wheels to her (on a car, bike, toys, stroller). Talk about how you will be making a car that has a wheel and axle and how you can use wind or air to make the car move. Discuss with your child how a wheel and axle is a simple machine.

2. Determine what you will use to make the body of the car, a tube or a box. If you use a box, you can later put weight in the box for further experiments and also dramatic play.

3. Determine what you will use for wheels and the axle.

4. Use either a skewer or straw as the base of your car, or punch a hole in the sides to push the axle through to support the car. Put wheels onto the axle. You will need to put something at the end of each axle to keep the wheels from sliding off (tape, another smaller wheel taped or glued on, a little playdough).

5. Determine the materials for the sail support and the sail itself and secure to the "car."

6. The car should now be ready to experiment with using different types of wind (blowing air through a straw, using a hand fan, using an electric fan, or outside wind).
7. Encourage your child's curiosity: What do you think will happen to your car if we provide more wind?
8. Encourage your child's critical-thinking skills: What can you tell me about wheels and axles?

Predict and Hypothesize

- Problem solve with your child: I wonder what will happen if we change the size of the wheels (size of sail, add weight, change the surface).
- Predict and hypothesize the answers to the questions. Test the hypotheses and record what you discover.

Did You Know?

- A rolling log, which is a primitive form of the wheel and axle, and a sloping hill, which is a naturally inclined plane, are early examples of simple machines.
- Wheels and axles changed our world and the ability to transport people and goods. Before wheels were invented, the transportation of goods was a major problem. Heavier goods took days to be transported from one place to other.

Add more STEAM activities:

Science—Discuss physics terms such as friction, wind, and air resistance. Look around when you travel and note the different types of wheels and axles that help people every day.

Technology—Record a video of your wind-powered car and narrate what you see happening.

Arts—Decorate your car.

Math—Measure and record the distance cars will go with different types of wind.

Simple Machines (Pulley)— Lift and Lower ❯

Children will assist in building a lever to lift and lower items to gain an understanding of the mechanical pulley.

Talk Like Engineers!

- **Effort**—the amount of force required to lift an object
- **Force**—a push or pull on an object; in this case, how hard you pull on the rope
- **Gravity**—a force that pulls things toward Earth
- **Load**—the weight of an object
- **Pulley**—a wheel with a grooved rim around which a cord passes; often used to raise heavy weights

What You Need

- Rope/string
- Empty ribbon spool (or, if not available, use a carabiner for rope to slide through)
- Small dowel if you are able to use a spool or wheel
- Carabiner
- Bucket or paint pail
- Apparatus or area to lift (you can build or use stair railing or limb of a tree)
- STEAM journal

How to Do It

1. Engage your child by asking, "What can you tell me about lifting a flag on a flagpole?" Talk about how you will be making a homemade pulley, a simple machine that can be used for lifting and lowering a load. There are many videos available on homemade pulleys, so you may want to research further with your child.
2. First, determine the area you will use for lifting and if you need to make an apparatus. You can also work in a stair area or with a tree limb.

3. Secure a bucket (you can use a carabiner or tie it) to the end of the rope. Make sure you have adequate rope to pull your load to the top of the spool.

4. Find a spool or wheel to be used. If you do not have a spool, you could use a carabiner or put the rope directly over the lifting apparatus.

5. Put a load in the bucket and pull on the rope to lift the load. Then lower the load back to the ground.

6. Encourage your child's curiosity: What would happen if you let the string go before lowering it back to the ground?

7. Encourage your child's critical-thinking skills: What can you tell me about a homemade pulley?

Predict and Hypothesize

- Problem solve with your child: I wonder what will happen if we add more weight into the bucket.
- Predict and hypothesize the answer to the question. Test the hypothesis and record what you discover.

Add more STEAM activities:

Science—Discuss physics terms of load, pulley, and force. Try different weights, pulling from different angles, and adding more than one wheel as a pulley.

Technology—Make a video of your pulley.

Arts—Draw pictures of pulleys you see in and outside your house.

Math—Record the weight of items to be lifted and how fast they fall to the ground if you let go of the rope.

Did You Know?

The exact origins of the pulley are not known. Around 1500 BC, the Mesopotamians are believed to have used rope pulleys to hoist water. The first documented compound pulley machine was developed by Archimedes, a Greek mathematician and inventor.

Simple Machines (Ramp/Incline)—Toy Cars ❯

Children will explore friction, incline, and acceleration by racing cars down ramps to further their understanding of inclines.

 Talk Like Engineers!

- **Air resistance**—a pushing force that slows things down
- **Friction**—the resistance of motion when one object rubs against the other; in this case, the resistance of the car wheels when moving over the inclined surface
- **Gravity**—a force that pulls things toward Earth; in this case, it causes the car to go down the ramp
- **Inclined plane**—a sloping ramp that makes it easier to move things up or down
- **Texture**—the feel of a surface

What You Need

- Materials to make ramps—wood planks may be best, but you can also use cardboard or other materials
- Variety of toy cars
- Variety of textured materials to create friction (sandpaper, rubbery shelf liner, carpet, foil, wax paper, sand, and so on)
- Tape to secure materials to ramp if needed
- Stopwatch and measuring tape
- STEAM journal

How to Do It

1. Tell your child that you will be experimenting with ramps and toy cars. Talk about how a ramp/inclined plane is a simple machine. If needed, look up images or videos about friction and ramps/inclines.

2. Determine how you will make your ramps—material of ramp(s), how many ramps you want to have available—(at least two should be constructed so comparisons can be made). Also determine how you will elevate the ramps and be able to change the angle of the incline and determine what materials you will use to provide friction.
3. Make the first ramp with no materials used for resistance. Experiment with this first ramp to determine which ramp angles are faster or slower and which cars move faster or slower (longer, shorter, heavy, or light cars).
4. Move on to making the textured ramps. Discuss friction and experiment with one textured ramp at a time.
5. At the same time, send similar toy cars down the ramp with no texture and with texture. Discuss how they are different.
6. Try different textures and discuss each of them. You may start to use the stopwatch and the measuring tape to show which car goes farther after they come off the ramp.
7. Explore changing the angle, the surface, and the toy car.
8. Encourage your child's curiosity: Why do you think some cars go farther than other cars?
9. Encourage your child's critical-thinking skills: What can you tell me about toy cars going down a ramp?

Predict and Hypothesize

- Problem solve with your child: I wonder what will happen if we launch the same cars but change the height of the incline.
- Predict and hypothesize the answer to the question. Test the hypothesis and record what you discover.

Did You Know?

Inclined planes have been used by people since prehistoric times to move heavy objects. The sloping roads and causeways built by ancient civilizations, such as the Romans, are examples of early inclined planes that have survived and show that they understood the value of this device for moving things uphill.

Add more STEAM activities:

Science—Discuss physics terms such as friction, inclines, and gravity. Look around when you travel and note the different types of inclined planes that help people every day.

Technology—Make a video of your toy cars and ramps and narrate what you see happening.

Arts—Make pictures of your results.

Math—Record the weight of items, height of incline, and compare how fast and/or how far they traveled.

Simple Machines (Screw)— Using a Screwdriver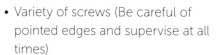

Children will experiment with using a screwdriver with different types of screws.

 ## Talk Like Engineers!

- **Inclined plane**—a sloping ramp that makes it easier to move things up or down
- **Screw**—an object with raised threads to help join or hold things together; an inclined plane wrapped around a cylinder used to hold things together

What You Need

- Variety of screws (Be careful of pointed edges and supervise at all times)
- Nails (May need a hammer, which is a lever)
- Screwdriver (A ratcheting screwdriver may be easier to use)
- Wood or cardboard (surfaces to "screw" together)
  ⚠ Safety Note: Nails and screws can be dangerous for small children. Closely supervise children with these small parts.
- STEAM journal

How to Do It

1. Prepare a variety of nails and screws for your child to see, and ask, "What can you tell me about these nails and screws?" Tell your child that you will be joining two surfaces together. Talk about how a screw is a simple machine.

2. First, invite your child to explore the use of a screwdriver with different types of screws and by screwing them into a surface (either scrap wood or thick cardboard). Make sure you place them on something that cannot be damaged.

3. Get your two surfaces that you plan to join together. First, try putting a nail through both surfaces.

4. Try to pull the two surfaces apart.

5. Next, try joining the surfaces with a screw and try pulling the surfaces apart.

6. Discuss what happens.

7. Encourage your child's curiosity: What do you think will happen if we use nails and not screws when building a structure?

8. Encourage your child's critical-thinking skills: What can you tell me about using screws?

Predict and Hypothesize

- Problem solve with your child: I wonder what will happen if we use different types of screws (with threads closer together or farther apart).
- Predict and hypothesize the answer to the questios. Test the hypothesis and record what you discover.

Add more STEAM activities:

Science—Experiment with plastic containers. You will need one with a screw top and one with a snap-on lid. Fill both with water and throw as far as you can outside on a sidewalk. What happens?

Technology—Make a video or take pictures of the objects around the house that have screws.

Arts—Make drawings of things that have some type of screw.

Math—Count the number of turns to get a screw to tighten.

Did You Know?
- Most historians believe the screw to be a Greek invention, likely by the third century BC.
- In the first century BC, wooden screws were commonly used throughout the Mediterranean world to press olive oil and wine.
- The screwdriver was invented in France or Germany in the fifteenth century.

Simple Machines (Wedge)— Will It Cut It? 〉

Children will experiment with a wedge to learn more about simple machinery.

 ## Talk Like Engineers!

- **Inclined plane**—a sloping ramp that makes it easier to move things up for down
- **Wedge**—a piece of a substance (such as wood or iron) that tapers to a thin edge and is used for splitting wood and rocks, raising heavy bodies, or for tightening by being driven into something (for example, ax, shovel, front of a ship, door stop, pointed end of a nail, knife, scissors, fingernail, fork, teeth)

What You Need
- Substances to cut (clay, apple, bread, cheese, cardboard, paper)
- Tools that will cut (scissors, butter knife, shovel, fork)
  ⚠ Safety Note: Be careful of any with very sharp edges.
- STEAM journal

How to Do It

1. Begin a conversation about simple machines by asking your child, "What can you tell me about cutting things?" Talk about how a wedge is a simple machine and tool for making work easier.
2. You may want to look up videos online about wedges and discuss with your child what she notices about them.
3. Assist your child as she works to discover what type of wedge is best for each job.
4. Use an apple, clay, or piece of cheese and ask your child what tool would be better to divide or cut it up into smaller pieces. She will probably say a knife. Show her how to cut it up and, if you have a safe knife (butter or plastic knife), let her try it.
5. Have a piece of cut-up apple or cheese and ask whether it would be easier to pick it up with a fork or a spoon and let her try it. Discuss what happens.
6. Use paper and ask what would be the best way to divide the paper. She will probably say scissors. Show her how to cut it up, and if you have safe scissors, let her try it.

7. Encourage your child's curiosity: What do you think will happen if we use a plastic knife to cut the apple?
8. Encourage your child's critical-thinking skills: What can you tell me about using wedges or things that cut or separate pieces?

Predict and Hypothesize

- Problem solve with your child: I wonder what will happen if we use different types of knives to cut through a piece of steak (use plastic knife, bread knife, smooth sharp knife, and serrated knife). ⚠ **Safety Note: Sharp knives should be used by adults only.**
- Predict and hypothesize the answers to the questions. Test the hypotheses and record what you discover.

Did You Know?

- Wedges have been around for thousands of years and were first made of stone.
- The origin of the wedge is not known. In ancient Egyptian quarries, bronze wedges were used to break away blocks of stone to use in construction. Wooden wedges that swelled after being saturated with water were also used around this time.

Add more STEAM activities:

Science—Discuss the other types of wedges you find to help do work and how different force might be used.
Technology—Make a video or take pictures of objects around the house that are wedges.
Arts—Utilize different examples of wedge-type scissors to get unique designs.
Math—Sort the different types of wedges used for work.

Simple Machines—(Review) Scavenger Hunt ❯

Children will go on a scavenger hunt in search of simple machines, which will be a precursor for understanding many engineering, math, and physics concepts.

What You Need

- Variety of simple machines (some suggestions: screw, toy with wheels, shovel, child-safe scissors, ladder, ramp, blinds)
- Recording sheet
- STEAM journal

 ## Talk Like Engineers!

- **Inclined plane**—a sloping ramp that makes it easier to move things up or down
- **Lever**—a stiff bar that rests on a support (fulcrum) to lift or move loads; for example, seesaw or crowbar
- **Machine**—a piece of equipment with moving parts that performs work when it is given power
- **Pulley**—a wheel or set of wheels that is used with a rope or chain to lift or lower heavy objects
- **Screw**—a simple machine consisting of an inclined plane spiraled around a cylinder
- **Wedge**— a piece of a substance (such as wood or iron) that tapers to a thin edge and is used for splitting wood and rocks, raising heavy bodies, or for tightening by being driven into something (ax, shovel, front of a ship, door stop, pointed end of a nail, knife, scissors, fingernail, fork)
- **Wheel and axle**—a simple lifting machine consisting of a rope that unwinds from a wheel onto a cylindrical drum or shaft joined to the wheel to provide mechanical advantage

How to Do It

1. Stimulate your child's curiosity by asking, "What are some things in our home that make it easier for us to do work?" You may want to start with a few examples—a ladder to get on the roof, scissors to cut paper, a lightbulb to screw into the lamp, and so on.
2. Introduce children to the six simple machines with a scavenger hunt.

Scavenger Hunt Ideas:

This list will get you started but make up your own for fun. Place the clues in a box and pull out one at a time. Give her clues with descriptive words (silver, round, and so on). Let her know she is getting closer or how many steps away she is.

- This simple machine is a wedge and is used to eat food and can be found in the kitchen (fork or knife).
- This simple machine is a wheel and axle and is used to open a door (doorknob).
- This simple machine is a screw and is used for light (lightbulb).
- This simple machine is an incline and is used to get up into the attic (ladder).
- This simple machine is called a pulley and is used to raise something to see outside (blinds).
- This simple machine is called a lever and helps you open a drink (can opener).

3. Encourage your child's curiosity: Why do you think an incline/ramp is needed for wheelchairs?
4. Encourage your child's critical-thinking skills: What can you tell me about simple machines?

Predict and Hypothesize

- Problem solve with your child: I wonder if other objects that are not round could be used to roll in a wheel and axle.
- Predict and hypothesize the answer to the question. Test the hypothesis and record what you discover.

Add more STEAM activities:

Science—Go to a playground or on a field trip and make notes on all the simple machines.

Technology—Make a video about the simple machines in your own home.

Engineering—Build a race car center using as many of the simple machines as possible [Ideas: Roll the car up to the ramp (pulley); put pieces together (screw); view tires on cars (the wheel and axle; lift cars into the apparatus for pulley (lever); use a wedge to cut apart materials to make the center].

Arts—Make your own chart about simple machines. You may want to cut pictures out of magazines.

Did You Know?

- Simple machines are just that: the simplest form of tool to accomplish something faster or better.
- There are six basic simple machines: the lever, the wheel and axle, the inclined plane, the wedge, the pulley, and the screw. Several of these simple machines are related to each other, but each has a specific purpose in the world of doing work.

ART

Darker and Lighter— Shadow Drawing ❯

Explore the different shapes created by sunlight at different times of day. Children will also explore light and shadow.

Talk Like Artists!

- **Dark**—without or partially without light
- **Light**—the bright form of energy given off by something (as the sun) that makes it possible to see
- **Shadow**—an area of darkness created when a source of light is blocked
- **Sun**—the star that Earth moves around and that gives Earth heat and light

How to Do It

1. Begin by asking your child some questions about light, such as "What is light? What is dark? What can you tell me about shadows?"
2. You may want to look up images of light, dark, and shadow online to further your child's understanding of these concepts. Talk about what you notice about the different terms.
3. Perform the experiment in early morning or late afternoon. Wear sunglasses and a hat.
4. Place the toy or other object on the paper.
5. Trace the outline of the shadow on the paper.
6. Encourage your child's curiosity: Are the shadows bigger, the same size, or smaller than the toy or object? When you rotate the toy/object, what happens to the shadow?
7. Encourage your child's critical-thinking skills: What can you tell me about shadows?

Predict and Hypothesize

- Problem solve with your child: I wonder what will happen if we trace the shadows at different times of the day or even at night.
- Try tracing objects at different times of day to predict and make a hypothesis about what will happen. Test the hypothesis by measuring the same object at different times. Chart what you discover.

What You Need

- Toys or another object to make a shadow
- Paper
- Marker
- Sunglasses/hat ⚠ Safety Note: Do not look directly into the sun.
- STEAM journal

Add more STEAM activities:

Science—Discuss how light travels in a straight line until it hits an object. When an object blocks out part of the light, the rest of the light keeps going. Discuss how shadows look different at different times of day because the sun's position changes. Discuss how shadows may be seen due to the moon at night.

Technology—Take pictures in early morning or late afternoon and discuss the shadows that can be seen in the pictures.

Engineering—Use other light sources to see if you can make a shadow.

Math—Take the drawings from different times of the day and measure the length of the shadow. Make a line chart that shows how the shadow may change. Try using a lamp and making different shapes on the wall.

Did You Know?

- Kumi Yamashita, a sculptor, constructs art using various materials and places them at a distance from light to create shadows.
- Typically, shadows are overlooked because we tend to pay attention to whatever is casting them. In the case of works of art, however, the roles have been reversed, and the shadow has become the main focus.

Texture—Sense of Feel ❯

Utilizing different materials, children will identify textures including soft, rough, smooth, hard, bumpy, or irregular.

 Talk Like Artists!

- **Bumpy**—having an uneven and irregular surface
- **Feel**—the act of touching something to examine it
- **Hard**—something that is solid or firm and not easily compressed
- **Rough**—having a coarse or irregular surface
- **Smooth**—having an even surface with no lumps or rough areas
- **Surface**—the outside part of an object
- **Texture**—the feel of a surface

What You Need

- Paper
- Marker
- Scissors
- Glue
- Pompom or cotton ball
- Shelf liner
- Sandpaper
- Metal washers or uncooked pasta
- Small rocks or sticks
- STEAM journal

How to Do It

1. Ask your child to touch different objects (face, beard, pillow, and so on) and describe the feeling. "What can you tell me about a rough (smooth, hard, bumpy) surface?" Talk about touch and feel, which is one of the five senses.
2. With your child, prepare to make a paper "hand" with different textures.
3. Help your child trace his hand and then make a cutout of the hand.
4. Glue a different object on each finger of the cutout (soft, smooth, rough, hard, bumpy).
5. Label the different fingers with the correct term for touch.
6. Encourage your child's curiosity: I wonder what each of the fingers would feel like if you rubbed them against your skin.
7. Encourage your child's critical-thinking skills: What can you tell me about the sense of touch?

Did You Know?

Artist Nick Cave's Soundsuits are wearable art made of many different textures. The various textures alter the sounds the suits make when worn.

Predict and Hypothesize

- Problem solve with your child: I wonder how the texture of household items such as the sofa, carpet, tile, dishes, and houseplants would feel.
- Predict and hypothesize the answer to the question. Test the hypothesis and chart what you discover.

Add more **STEAM** activities:

Science—Discuss objects or items found in nature and how they may feel.

Technology—Take pictures of items with different textures and surfaces and make a texture book.

Engineering—Use a ramp to test cars to see on which surface the cars will go the fastest.

Math—From the Predict and Hypothesize experiment, place items on a graph to determine how many items were soft or hard.

Did You Know?

- Texture is the perceived surface quality of a work of art. It is an element of two-dimensional and three-dimensional designs and is distinguished by its perceived visual and physical properties.
- The actual surface texture needs to either be felt or seen with light raking across its surface to make texture visible. Painters are most likely to take advantage of this to give their painting's surface a realistic look. Some painters add sand to their paint to make a more tactile texture.

Color Mixing—Making Icing ❯

Children will learn about primary and secondary colors by making icing for cookies.

 Talk Like Artists!

- **Mixing**—combining two or more ingredients
- **Primary colors**—the colors red, yellow, and blue
- **Secondary colors**—the colors orange, green, and purple; made by mixing two primary colors

What You Need

- Vanilla frosting
- Food coloring (red, yellow, and blue)
- Plain vanilla cookies
- Measuring spoons
- Bowls
- Spoons or wooden craft sticks for stirring
- Plates
- STEAM journal

How to Do It

1. Find some colorful items and ask your child, "What can you tell me about colors?" Ask him to name different colors. "Can you point out and show me something that is red or yellow or blue? Those colors are called primary colors. If we mix those colors together we get secondary or other colors."
2. Discuss your child's observations on colors and ask him questions throughout the activity.
3. Put white icing into three bowls.
4. Add red food coloring to one bowl, yellow food coloring to another bowl, and blue food coloring to the last bowl. Explain to your child that these are the primary colors.

5. Have your child use measuring spoons to put an equal amount of two primary colors together in a new bowl and mix them together.
6. Continue to add two primary colors in new bowls (red + yellow = orange; red + blue = purple; yellow + blue = green).
7. Use the icing to spread on the cookies and enjoy.
8. Encourage your child's curiosity: I wonder if the icing will taste the same since it is different colors?
9. Encourage your child's critical-thinking skills: What can you tell me about mixing colors?

Predict and Hypothesize

- Problem solve with your child: I wonder what would happen if we mixed more of one color than the other color.
- Predict and hypothesize the answer to the question. Test the hypothesis and chart what you discover.

Did You Know?

In the visual arts, color theory is a body of guidance to mixing colors. A color circle, based on primary colors of red, yellow, and blue, is traditionally used in the field of art. Sir Isaac Newton developed the first circular diagram of colors in 1666. Since then, scientists and artists have studied and designed numerous variations of this concept.

Add more STEAM activities:

Science—Try mixing colors with other types of substances (such as water, shaving cream, sand, or homemade playdough).

Technology—Take pictures of items of different colors and indicate whether they are primary or secondary colors.

Engineering—Use colored playdough and wooden craft sticks to make a color wheel.

Math—Make a chart with primary colors across the top and other colors listed. Note how many drops of red, yellow, or blue are needed to make that color; for example, orange might be one red and two drops of yellow.

Patterns—Making a Caterpillar »

Children will learn about making patterns as they make a caterpillar out of colored paper.

Talk Like Artists

- **Design**—to create, fashion, execute, or construct according to plan
- **Duplicate**—make an exact copy of something
- **Pattern**—a repeated form or design that is especially used for decoration

What You Need

- Red, yellow, and blue construction paper
- Scissors
- Glue
- Crayons
- Large piece of paper
- STEAM journal

How to Do It

1. Look with your child to find patterns around him (clothing, dishes, furniture, book covers). Ask, "What can you tell me about patterns?" You may need to give your child an example to get him started.
2. Listen to your child's ideas about patterns and talk about them as you make a caterpillar.

3. Cut out circles from the three colors of construction paper.
4. Have him lay out a pattern (blue, yellow, red—blue, yellow, red—and so on).
5. Once he has a pattern, he can glue it on the larger paper to make a caterpillar.
6. Use crayons to color legs and antennae.
7. Encourage your child's curiosity: I wonder if we changed the order of the colors or the number of colors, then repeated them, would we still have a pattern?
8. Encourage your child's critical-thinking skills: What can you tell me about patterns?

Predict and Hypothesize

- Problem solve with your child: I wonder if we looked at pictures of real caterpillars if we would find a pattern.
- Predict and hypothesize the answer to the question. Test the hypothesis and chart what you discover.

Add more STEAM activities:

Science—Look for shapes in nature. Search for other patterns in nature.

Technology—Take pictures of patterns that you find in nature.

Engineering—Build a structure with a pattern using colored blocks or blocks of different shapes. Make a necklace by using different colors in a pattern.

Math—Show patterns with shapes in math—triangle, square, circle—triangle, square, _____. (What comes next?)

Did You Know?

- Artist Antonio Gaudí, who was fascinated by patterns in nature, transformed his city of Barcelona into an art gallery.
- All pattern artists use patterns in their art. The medium or technique is not important, as long as they employ a combination of elements or shapes repeated in a recurring and regular arrangement.

Three-Dimensional Art— Making a Tree 》

Children will learn about three-dimensional art by making a paper tree.

What You Need

- Brown paper lunch bag
- Tissue paper (fall colors of brown, red, and yellow)
- Scissors
- Glue
- STEAM journal

 Talk Like Artists!

- **Autumn**—the season of the year between summer and winter; the weather gets cooler
- **Leaf**—part of the plant that grows from a stem
- **Three-dimensional art**—art that has height, width, and depth
- **Tree**—a woody perennial plant having a single, main stem generally with few or no branches on its lower part
- **Two-dimensional art**—any artwork on a flat surface (painting, drawings, and so on)

How to Do It

1. If possible, look at some leaves to compare color and size. Ask your child, "What can you tell me about leaves on trees?" Talk with your child about how many leaves change colors in the fall.
2. Show your child a picture of a tree and discuss that the picture is two dimensional or "flat."
3. Tell your child that you are going to make a three-dimensional tree.

4. Take the bag and make many cuts from the top to approximately two-thirds of bag (to seam or fold).
5. Open the bag (you may want to put something in the bottom of the bag to give some weight to assist with the bag staying upright).
6. Take the top part of the bag and carefully twist just above the seam.
7. To form branches, gather two or three strips at a time and twist together.
8. Cut and glue small pieces of tissue paper onto the branches.
9. Encourage your child's curiosity: Which tree looks more real—the two-dimensional or three-dimensional tree?
10. Encourage your child's critical-thinking skills: What can you tell me about making a three-dimensional tree?

Predict and Hypothesize
- Problem solve with your child: I wonder if we can collect real leaves and add them to our tree.
- Predict and hypothesize the answer to the question. Test the hypothesis by adding leaves and chart what you discover.

Add more STEAM activities:
Science—Research and discuss seasons and why leaves change colors.

Technology—Review videos for children on changing seasons and leaves changing colors.

Engineering—Draw pictures in two dimensions, then try to build a three-dimensional structure.

Math—Measure the height, width, and depth of objects.

Did You Know?
Three-dimensional art is observed in terms of its height, width, and depth. It is not flat like two-dimensional art, which consists of paintings, drawings, and photographs. Pottery and sculpture are examples of three-dimensional art.

Watercolor Butterflies ❯

Children will use watercolor paints to create butterflies to learn more about the anatomy of the butterfly.

 Talk Like Artists!

What You Need
- Coffee filters
- Watercolor paints
- Pipe cleaners
- Paint brushes
- Fishing line
- STEAM journal

- **Antennae**—one of a pair of slender, movable, segmented sensory organs on the head of insects that may be used for smelling and sometimes taste and hearing
- **Butterfly**—an insect with a long, thin body and brightly colored wings that flies mostly during the day
- **Life cycle**—a series of changes that happen to a living thing from the beginning of its life
- **Wings**—paired appendages that help some animals, such as butterflies, fly

How to Do It

1. Start a discussion with your child about butterflies, and ask, "What can you tell me about butterflies?"
2. Listen to your child's ideas and talk about them. You may want to look up images of different butterflies to help your child visualize the many varieties.
3. Open up a coffee filter and spread it flat on the painting surface.
4. Using the brush and watercolors, paint the entire surface. Make sure something is under the filter since the watercolors will pass through the filter. Be careful to not get it too wet and rip/shred the filter.
5. Allow the filter to dry (at least twenty minutes).
6. Gather the filter in the middle and hold together.
7. Use a pipe cleaner to make and hold the folded part of the insect body together.
8. To make the antennae, take a pipe cleaner and fold it in half. Position it so that it's in the center of the coffee filter. Twist the pipe cleaner to hold the coffee filter together and then form the antennae.
9. Using the fishing line, hang your butterflies.
10. Encourage your child's curiosity: What do you think will happen if we use different colors on our filters to make the wings?
11. Encourage your child's critical-thinking skills: What can you tell me about butterflies?

Predict and Hypothesize

- Problem solve with your child: I wonder what will happen if we hang our butterfly out in the wind.
- Predict and hypothesize the answer to the question. Test the hypothesis and record what you discover.

Add more STEAM activities:

Science—Discuss the life cycle of a butterfly (from egg, to caterpillar, to butterfly).

Technology—Review videos for children about the life cycle of a butterfly.

Engineering—Plan and create other types of butterflies.

Math—Visit a nursery or butterfly farm and count and sort the butterflies.

Did You Know?

- Watercolor is a painting method in which the paints are made of pigments suspended in a water-based solution. Watercolor refers to both the medium and the resulting artwork.
- Watercolor painting is extremely old, dating perhaps to the cave paintings of Paleolithic Europe, and has been used for manuscript illustration since at least ancient Egyptian times. Watercolor was especially popular in Europe in the Middle Ages.

Steady Beat—Rhythm Sticks ❯

This activity includes music, movement, and art as children use paper rhythm sticks to keep a steady beat.

 Talk Like Artists!

- **Beat**—a main accent in music
- **Sound**—vibrations that travel through the air or an object and can be heard with the ears
- **Steady**—a regular or even movement or sound

How to Do It

1. Clap your hands and invite your child to clap her hands too. The ability for children to keep a steady beat is an important developmental stage. Play some music and ask your child to clap to the steady beat. You may need to help him. You could also say a nursery rhyme and clap or pat the steady beat.
2. You may also want to look up music videos to help your child clap a steady beat. Note: There is a difference between a steady beat (X X X X) and a rhythmical pattern (X x/x X x/x), and children should learn steady beat first.
3. Collaborate with your child to make his own rhythm sticks.
4. First, lay the grocery bag out flat.
5. Tightly roll up the bag to make a "stick."
6. Put tape around the ends and the center of the "stick." You can also use duct tape and decorate the entire "stick" with colors or patterns.
7. Play a game called the echo game before using music. Begin by saying, "My turn," and tap a beat on the table or floor (one to four beats). Then say "your turn" and the child will repeat or "echo" the set of beats. Do this several times.
8. Next, identify a body part to tap on and chant and ask your child to join you in "saying and doing" (Example: knees, knees, knees, knees | knees, knees, knees, knees). This is done for eight counts.
9. Then move on to another body part for eight counts (shoulders, head, tummy, feet, and so on). This activity helps children develop a steady beat and learn their different body parts.
10. Next, play music and have your child tap his stick on the ground and/or march to the beat.
11. Encourage your child's curiosity: I wonder if there are other ways to keep steady beat.
12. Encourage your child's critical-thinking skills: What can you tell me about making rhythm sticks and steady beat?

Predict and Hypothesize

- Problem solve with your child: I wonder if we can listen to music and tap on one body part, then another, then another to make a dance.
- Predict and hypothesize the answer to the question. Record the different dance steps or pattern.

What You Need

- Brown grocery bag—regular size
- Tape
- Variety of music
- Duct tape (optional)
- Crayons or markers (optional)
- STEAM journal

Did You Know?

Clapsticks or clappers are a type of percussion instrument that originated to maintain rhythm in Australian Aboriginal music. Clapsticks are intended for striking one stick on another.

Add more STEAM activities:

Science—Have your child put his hands on his neck and hum. Now have him talk. Ask him about the vibration and explain that it is vibration and sound waves that make sound.

Technology—Try a music app (like GarageBand) to make music.

Engineering—Plan and create other musical instruments to keep the steady beat (shakers, drums, bells).

Math—Count out number of beats (usually best in fours).

Dance Painting with Feet ❯

Your child will paint with his feet in this activity, which includes music, dance, and art. Introduce your child to fast, slow, and freeze concepts of moving.

 ## Talk Like Artists!

- **Dance**—to move one's body rhythmically usually to music
- **Fast**—with great speed
- **Slow**—at a low speed
- **Speed**—the rate at which something moves
- **Stop**—to cease moving

What You Need
- Large sheet of paper
- Paint (perhaps more than one color)
- Container big enough for feet to step into (a pan, Frisbee, bin)
- Equipment and/or area to clean feet
- Music
- STEAM journal

How to Do It

1. Spark interest by asking your child, "What can you tell me about painting with your feet?" Tell your child that you will be able to step into some paint and then dance on the paper.
2. Talk with your child about what you notice about dance and movement as you perform the activity.
3. Have paper ready and close to the container with the paint.
4. Have your child step into the paint and then onto the paper.
5. Play some music and ask your child to move to the music. When you stop the music, he should stop moving (freeze, be a statue).

6. Play music with different tempos (fast, slow) and have him dance. You may want to have different colors of paint available. You may suggest ways to move/dance (tiptoes, heels, twist, go in a circle).
7. Clean up feet and containers and let the paper dry. 💡 **Tip: The painted paper can then be used to wrap gifts at a later date.**
8. Encourage your child's curiosity: I wonder if we change how we move our feet if it will change the paint we see on the paper.
9. Encourage your child's critical-thinking skills: What can you tell me about dancing and painting with your feet?

Predict and Hypothesize

- Problem solve with your child: I wonder if we can identify where you were dancing fast and where you were dancing slow.
- Predict and hypothesize the answers to the questions. Test the hypotheses and record what you discover.

Add more STEAM activities:

Science—Discuss the physics of dance: force, gravity, and speed.

Technology—Make a video of parts of the dance so a connection can be made between the speed and dance movements to the paint on the paper.

Engineering—Plan and create other dance patterns.

Math—Count how many times you step to fast music versus slow music.

Making Faces 》

This art activity utilizes household materials to make a face to help children learn about feelings and emotions.

What You Need

- Construction paper or felt
- Household materials (buttons, pipe cleaners, yarn, string, shapes, toothpicks)
- Mirror
- Glue
- STEAM journal

 Talk Like Artists!

- **Face**—the front part of the head that in humans extends from the forehead to the chin and includes the mouth, nose, cheeks, and eyes
- **Feelings**—emotional states or reactions
- **Happy**—feeling pleasure and enjoyment
- **Mad**—very angry
- **Sad**—affected with or expressive of grief or unhappiness

How to Do It

1. Begin by saying, "Show me how your face looks when you are happy. Show me how your face looks when you are sad. Show me how your face looks when you are angry." If he doesn't understand, give him a situation and show him how your face would look. Example: "I am happy when I can go play and I smile." Discuss how you can look at someone's face and sometimes know how he feels or understand his feelings. Talk with your child about how everyone has different emotions.
2. You may want to find images of facial expressions to help him understand what someone could be feeling with certain expressions. Continue to talk to him about feelings and emotions as you conduct the activity.
3. Cut out an oval to be the face. A texture like felt might keep objects from rolling off the face.
4. Your child will build the face on her oval felt or construction paper.
5. Ask your child to first make a happy face with the various materials. ⚠ **Safety Note: Closely supervise your child as he works with these loose parts.**
6. Then ask him how he would change the face to be a sad face.

7. Your child may want to make more than one face, so have different cut-out ovals for him to use. He can glue down and save or display the different faces with emotions.
8. Encourage your child's curiosity: Look in the mirror and show me the different facial expressions you can make.
9. Encourage your child's critical-thinking skills: What can you tell me about feelings?

Predict and Hypothesize

- Problem solve with your child: I wonder if we look through some books whether we can find different expressions on the faces.
- Predict and hypothesize the answer to the question. Test the hypothesis and record what you discover.

Add more STEAM activities:

Science—Discuss how muscles are used in the face to change expressions. Invite your child to move the parts of her face in different ways.

Technology—Take pictures of different expressions.

Engineering—Plan and create faces with other materials.

Math—Keep a chart to see what feelings/faces you had for part of the day.

Did You Know?

Children who can understand and manage their feelings, calm themselves, and enjoy their experiences are more likely to develop a positive sense of self and be confident and curious learners. Children develop their emotional skills through their relationships with others, such as their parents and caretakers. The ability to show emotions in a fun way and then discuss feelings is an important part of development.

Musical Jars ❯

In this activity, your child will make his own musical instruments with water and glass containers.

 Talk Like Artists!

- **Measure**—to find out the size, length, or amount of something
- **Musical instrument**—a device, such as a violin, piano, or flute, used to make music
- **Sound**—a particular auditory impression

What You Need

- Identical glass containers
- Water
- Food coloring (optional)
- Measuring cup
- Spoon or other object (to use to strike glass)
- Sound checklist
- STEAM journal

How to Do It

1. Going on a sound walk is a great way to introduce sounds. Create a list of sounds that you can hear such as dog barks, planes, cars, or machines to discover soft and loud sounds, short and long sounds, and so on.
2. There are many resources available, so you may want to find videos about making sounds with musical jars. Talk with your child about different sounds and discuss what he likes to hear.
3. To conduct your experiment with sounds, place six to eight glasses in a row.
4. In the first glass, add 1/8 cup of water. Let your child help you measure with the measuring cups.

5. In the next cup, put in 1/4 cup of water. It may be best to measure 1/8 cup and pour it in two times to use math.
6. Keep adding more water to each glass container in 1/8 cup increments.
7. Let your child "play" the musical instruments. You might make up a song or rhythmical pattern.
8. Encourage your child's curiosity: What do you think would happen if we put more water in another glass?
9. Encourage your child's critical-thinking skills: What can you tell me about making music with water and glasses?

Predict and Hypothesize

- Problem solve with your child: I wonder if we can use other types of containers and make sound.
- Predict and hypothesize the answer to the question. Test the hypothesis and record what you discover.

Did You Know?
Music is a powerful tool that can help children learn new thinking skills. When children play with musical instruments, they explore cause and effect. Making musical instruments and exploring with them helps children learn how different instruments work and the different sounds they create.

Add more STEAM activities:

Science—Discuss how sound is made by vibration. Make a drum with plastic stretched across a can and cover the side of the can with paper. Use a fabric or a paper bag to cover the top of the drum.

Technology—Have your child speak into a recorder and try to make different types of sounds: whisper, talk, sing, speak higher, lower, louder, and softer. Show a video of sound waves and how they get bigger, smaller, closer together, or farther apart.

Engineering—Plan and create other musical instruments.

Math—Make a chart of the measurements or amount of water in each glass.

Making Suncatchers 〉

Children will create a suncatcher/wind chime decoration that will let sunlight filter through, which will help them learn about the sun's rays.

 Talk Like Artists!

- **Light**—the bright form of energy given off by something (as the sun) that makes it possible to see
- **Sun**—the star that Earth moves around and that gives Earth heat and light
- **Suncatcher**—a window ornament, especially of colored glass or paper
- **Transparent**—allows light to pass through so objects behind it are visible

What You Need

- Metal cookie cutters/molds
- Baking sheet
- Baking paper
- Plastic beads
- Drill or other device to make a hole into decoration (adult use only)
- String, yard, or fishing line
- Tree branch
- STEAM journal

How to Do It

1. Look through a window with your child and ask, "Why can we see through the window?" Tell him that the glass is transparent and allows the sun and light to pass through.
2. Listen to your child's ideas about light and conduct research online or in books to see stained glass windows or videos on making suncatchers.
3. To make your suncatcher, place baking paper on top of the baking sheet.
4. Lay out the cookie cutters or molds on the sheet.
5. Place beads into the mold, approximately two layers in the middle and one layer near the edge (place higher in the middle and stay a little away from the sides if possible).
6. Parents only: Place into a warm oven (180–200 C; 350–400 F) and bake until you can see the beads have melted. Do not allow children to reach into the oven, though you may want to watch from a safe distance as the beads melt through the oven window.
7. Once the beads have cooled, remove the decoration from the mold.
8. Drill a hole in the top for string or fishing line.
9. Hang from a tree branch.
10. Encourage your child's curiosity: What do you think will happen if we hold these decorations up to the light?
11. Encourage your child's critical-thinking skills: What can you tell me about the sun and suncatchers?

Predict and Hypothesize

- Problem solve with your child: What will happen if we make decorations that are different colors?
- Predict and hypothesize the answer to the question. Test the hypothesis and record what you discover.

Did You Know?

A suncatcher is a small, translucent ornament that is hung indoors at windows to "catch the light," which then disperses in colors. A suncatcher can be said to be the optical equivalent of a wind chime.

Add more STEAM activities:

Science—Discuss light and what happens if it goes through different colors of glass.

Technology—Look at videos of suncatchers or stained glass.

Engineering—Plan and create other items (perhaps shapes, animals, holiday decorations, a necklace, a mobile).

Math—Count the numbers or types of beads used in the mold.

Making Predictions— Sink or Float 〉

Children will predict which objects will sink or float in an experiment that will encourage learning about various measurements, such as mass, weight, and density.

What You Need

- Large container filled with water
- Variety of objects (plastic, wood, foam, metal, coins, food, feathers, and so on)
- Recording sheet
- STEAM journal

 Talk Like Mathematicians!

- **Buoyancy**—the power of a liquid to make something float
- **Density**—the distribution of a quantity (such as mass, electricity, or energy) per unit
- **Float**—something that rests in or on the surface of a fluid
- **Heavy**—of great mass or weight
- **Light**—having little weight
- **Mass**—a quantity of matter; weight
- **Predict**—foretell on the basis of observation, experience, or scientific reason
- **Sink**—to go down below the surface
- **Weight**—a unit of mass

How to Do It

1. Ask your child, "If I put a plastic duck in the water, would it sink or float? What about a marble?" Talk to your child about how a guess is also called a prediction.
2. Work with your child to make predictions by listing items on a sheet about what will sink or float.
3. Get a large container filled with water ready for the experiment.
4. Place a variety of objects next to the container.
5. Record each one on the chart.
6. Invite your child to touch and examine the objects. Talk to her about each item.
7. Ask your child to predict whether it will sink or float and record her guess.
8. Place the object on top of the water and record what happens.
9. Review the results together at the end of the experiment.
10. Encourage your child's curiosity: Why do so some objects float in water and why do some objects sink?
11. Encourage your child's critical-thinking skills: What can you tell me about floating and sinking in the water?

Sink or Float Predictions				
Object	What do you predict will happen?		What happened?	
	Sink	Float	Sink	Float
1.				
2.				
3.				
4.				
5.				
6.				
7.				
8.				

Predict and Hypothesize

- Problem solve with your child: What will happen if we select other objects and check to see if they will sink or float?
- Predict and hypothesize the answer to the question. Test the hypothesis and record what you discover.

Add more STEAM activities:

Science—Discuss the physics terms and try a liquid other than water (oil, alcohol, soda).

Technology—Make a video about the items that float or sink.

Engineering—Create a boat that floats and try adding weighted objects until it sinks.

Arts—Draw a picture with a water line and then draw the things that sink below the water and the objects that float on top of the water.

Did You Know?

- Whether an object floats or sinks depends on the object's density, not its weight. Things denser than water sink in water, while things having less mass than water float on it.
- Things float when they are less dense than the fluid in which they are sitting. This does not mean that an object has to be lighter than the fluid, as in the case of a boat; objects need to have a higher ratio of empty space to mass than the fluid.

Comparing—More or Less (Greater Than or Less Than) ❯

Children will compare and determine which group has more or less.

 Talk Like Mathematicians!

- **Compare**—to examine the character or qualities of something to discover resemblances or differences
- **Less**—a smaller quantity, number, or amount
- **More**—a greater quantity, number, or amount

How to Do It

1. Prepare two piles of cookies and engage your child's curiosity by asking, "Of the two piles of cookies, which pile contains more cookies?"
2. If your child is interested in learning more about comparisons, look up videos about children making comparisons in math.
3. Designate two areas in which you will put the items to compare.
4. Put your first items in two piles with unequal numbers in each pile (Example: four blocks and two blocks).
5. Ask your child to compare the piles and determine which has more.
6. Once she tells you her guess, lay each piece end to end to create a line of objects from each pile. Seeing which line is longer will help make the concept more concrete for your child.
7. Write down the number of pieces in each pile.
8. Continue with the comparison of items.
9. Encourage your child's curiosity: How can you figure out which group has more?
10. Encourage your child's critical-thinking skills: What can you tell me about comparing and counting?

Predict and Hypothesize

- Problem solve with your child: I wonder what will happen if we combine objects that are not the same. Can you guess which group had more?
- Predict and hypothesize the answers to the questions. Test the hypotheses and record what you discover.

Did You Know?

Child care providers and parents know that children understand the concepts "greater than," "less than," and "equal to" when they give children crackers and Jimmy says that Danny has more crackers than he does. Taking away crackers from Danny and giving them to Jimmy may not be popular with Danny, but if he understands the concepts of more than, less than, and equal to or the same as, this solution will be accepted as fair.

Add more STEAM activities:

Science—Discuss birds or other animals that you see outside. Try to determine whether there are more or fewer birds in one area compared to another area.

Technology—Try an app that provides opportunities to determine more or less.

Engineering—Create and build something with piles of blocks to show more or less. For example, what would happen if she put six blocks on one side and four on the other side. Would the roof be straight across?

Arts—Draw pictures of animals that have more legs than humans.

Sorting/Categorizing— Sounds All around Us ❯

What You Need
- Recording sheet
- STEAM journal

Children will listen to sounds and sort them into categories: human (voice or body sounds), animal, transportation, tools/equipment, other.

 Talk Like Mathematicians!

- **Categorize**—to put something into a group of similar things; sort
- **Compare**—to examine the character or qualities of something to discover resemblances or differences
- **Sound**—a particular auditory impression
- **Sound waves**—formed when a sound (vibration) is made and moves through the air, causing movement in the air particles. These particles bump into the particles close to them, which makes them vibrate too, causing them to bump

How to Do It

1. Begin by saying to your child, "Listen carefully—what do you hear?" Explain that you hear with your ears, and hearing is one of your five senses.
2. While inside, sit down and ask your child to close her eyes and tell you the sounds she is hearing.
3. You may also make some sounds for her to identify (hum, whistle, clap hands, snap fingers, whisper, sing, and so on).
4. Write the names of each sound she identifies on the sheet.
5. Once she opens her eyes, help her categorize each sound and put a check on the sheet.
6. To help develop vocabulary and observation skills, ask your child to describe the sounds she's heard. She may need some prompting with questions such as, "Was the sound low/high pitched? Was it a whisper? Was it soft or loud?
7. Encourage your child's curiosity: How did you focus to hear and identify the sounds?
8. Encourage your child's critical-thinking skills: What can you tell me about sounds around us?"

Sound	Human Voice or Body Noise	Animal	Trans- portation	Tools / Equipment	Other	Describe

Predict and Hypothesize

- Problem solve with your child: Do you think we would hear different things outside?
- Predict and hypothesize the answer to the question. Test the hypothesis and record what you discover.

Add more STEAM activities:

Science—Discuss sound and sound waves. Go on a listening walk.

Technology—Use a recorder and record different sounds.

Engineering—Create and build a device that will amplify sounds.

Arts—Draw pictures of different things that make sounds.

Did You Know?

A sound wave is caused by the movement of energy traveling through a medium, such as air, water, or any other liquid or solid matter, as it moves away from the source of the sound. The source is an object that causes a vibration, which creates outward movement in a wave pattern. The wave carries the sound energy through the medium, usually in all directions and less intensely as it moves farther from the source.

Roll the Cubes— Number Recognition and Physical Activity ❯

Children will roll cubes to enhance number recognition and physical activity.

What You Need

- 2 boxes or 12 pieces of square card stock
- Markers
- Tape
- STEAM journal

 Talk Like Mathematicians (and Scientists)!

- **Exercise**—physical activity that is done to become stronger and healthier
- **Heart**—the organ that pumps blood through veins and arteries
- **Muscles**—a body tissue that can contract and produce movement
- **Number recognition**—ability to identify or name numerals

How to Do It

1. Ask your child some questions, such as, "How many fingers am I holding up? How many ears do you have? We are going to play a game using numbers and exercise."
2. Listen to your child's ideas and talk about numbers (numbers 1, 2, 3, 4, 5, 6).
3. Use a box that is already square or make your own with card stock and tape. To make your own cubes, put two pieces of square card stock edge to edge and tape the edges. Continue until you have a four-sided square. Then tape one piece of card stock to create a top and one piece to create a bottom.
4. Repeat for the second cube.
5. To make a number cube, use a marker to write on each side numbers 1 through 6. You may also want to add the "dots" to correlate with that number.
6. To make a movement cube, use a marker to write six activities. The activities need to be those your child can count as she does the activity. Some suggestions include "Jump, stomp your feet, clap your hands, pat your legs, touch your toes, turn in a circle."
7. First roll the number cube and identify the number.

8. Roll the movement/exercise cube and explain that you will do the exercise the same number of times as the cube. Example: Roll the number 4, then jump four times.
9. Roll the two cubes again for the next exercise.
10. Encourage your child's curiosity: How did you know how many times to perform the exercise?
11. Encourage your child's critical-thinking skills: What can you tell me about using cubes for numbers and exercise?

Predict and Hypothesize

- Problem solve with your child: If we roll through the number cube five times, how many times would it land on number 1?
- Predict and hypothesize the answer to the question. Test the hypothesis and record what you discover.

Add more STEAM activities:

Science—Discuss which of the six activities increased the heart beat and breathing.

Technology—Try an app that you can place a finger on to measure your heartbeat.

Engineering—Create other options for the cubes (shapes to run and touch in the room, animal sounds to make, and so on).

Arts—Draw pictures of exercises.

Did You Know?

This game can also be used to talk about odds, making predictions, and probability. A prediction game allows users to guess at the outcome of future events. Because there are only six options on the cube, you can predict or chart the outcomes. Younger children may just enjoy the physical activity, but it's developmentally important for them to hear and practice number recognition.

Sorting Fun in the Supermarket ❭

What You Need
- Pencils
- Clipboard
- Scavenger hunt sheet
- Vegetables and fruits
- STEAM journal

Children will practice sorting skills by completing a scavenger hunt activity during a supermarket visit. At the end of the activity, children will be able to sort fruits and vegetables, a key math concept.

 Talk Like Mathematicians!

- **Count**—to add items together to find the total number
- **One-to-one correspondence**—to count one object at a time, without skipping other objects or counting an object more than once
- **Sort**—group items by specific characteristics

How to Do It

1. Prepare a scavenger hunt sheet with pictures of fruits and vegetables for your child prior to your supermarket visit.
2. Ask your child if she knows the difference between fruits and vegetables.
3. Explain to your child that you will be going on a scavenger hunt in the supermarket. Give your child the clipboard and the scavenger hunt sheet that you created.

4. Once you have found an item, encourage your child to mark it off, and, if possible, buy the item to explore.

5. Once you have completed the activity, tell your child that you will continue the activity at home.

6. Help her count the items one by one. Invite your child to observe and explore a fruit and a vegetable and to sort the items into two groups, fruits and vegetables.

7. Encourage your child's curiosity: Tell your child that the main difference between fruits and vegetables is that fruits have seeds while vegetables are from other plant parts, so they don't have seeds. How can we find out if it has seeds inside? Open up different fruits and vegetables to look for seeds. Then ask your child to predict whether the fruit or vegetable has seeds inside. Compare your child's predictions with the results.

8. Encourage your child's critical-thinking skills: Talk about the meaning of the word sorting. Tell your child that when we sort we put things that are alike together. What can you tell me about sorting different fruits and vegetables?

Predict and Hypothesize

- Problem solve with your child: Do you think we could find out how many seeds are inside the fruit?
- Predict and hypothesize the answer to the question. Test the hypothesis and record what you discover.

Add more **STEAM** activities:

Science—Learn about growing plants.

Technology—Plant a seed and use pictures to document the growth.

Engineering—Use an iPad to record the growth from seed to plant.

Arts—Create the scavenger hunt recording sheet with precut magazine pictures and glue them on paper.

Did You Know?

Sorting is a beginning math skill. By sorting, children understand that things are alike and different and that they can belong and be organized into certain groups. Getting practice with sorting at an early age is important for developing numerical concepts and grouping numbers and sets when they're older. This type of thinking starts children on the path of applying logic to objects, mathematical concepts, and everyday life in general.

Nature Walk Adventures❯

Math concepts are formed through concrete experiences. Sorting is a foundational skill that allows children to explore materials, objects, and nature, and to sort according to different features. Children will practice sorting leaves by shape after a nature walk.

What You Need

- Paper bags to gather leaves
- Pencils
- Clipboard
- Different leaves and shapes
- STEAM journal

 Talk Like Mathematicians!

- **Classify**—to arrange people or things into groups based on ways that they are alike
- **Count**—to add people or things together to find the total number
- **Leaf**—one of the flat and typically green parts of a plant that grow from a stem or twig
- **Leaf attributes**—thin, wide, tall, short, heart-shaped, smooth, flat
- **Match**—to group items by identical characteristics
- **Sort**—group items by specific characteristics

How to Do It

1. Before you begin, ask your child if all leaves look the same. Talk with your child about the many different shapes and sizes in nature.
2. Explain to your child that you will be going on a nature walk to gather leaves to explore. Give her a paper bag to gather items. Encourage her to collect different leaves for further exploration.
3. Once you have gathered different types of leaves, tell your child that you will continue the activity at home.
4. Together, count how many items were collected and invite her to examine the leaves one by one. Tell her that there are different ways the leaves can be grouped and ask her for suggestions on ways to group them (size, shape, color).
5. Allow your child to observe and explore the leaves and decide what group they belong to.
6. Encourage your child's curiosity: Do all the trees have the same leaves? Do leaves have things in common? Do you think that all leaves have the same size? Observing leaves will allow you to practice observation skills.
7. Encourage your child's critical-thinking skills: What can you tell me about how we can find out which leaf is bigger?

Predict and Hypothesize

- Problem solve with your child: Do you think we could find out how long this leaf is? This is a great opportunity to allow children to learn about different measuring tools to compare leaves. Your child can measure the leaf with familiar units first (such as Unifix cubes, paper clips, or any other familiar unit) and later with rulers.
- Predict and hypothesize the answer to the question. Test the hypothesis and record what you discover.

Add more STEAM activities:

Science—Learn about the parts of a leaf and use your five senses to learn about leaves.
Technology—Plant a seed and use pictures to document the growth.
Engineering—Use a story kit app to explain the job of a leaf.
Arts—Make leaf collages.

Did You Know?

Many studies and reports, campaigns, and back-to-nature movements emphasize that children need nature and time outdoors, whether for their emotional well-being, improving their learning abilities, increasing their attentiveness, reducing stress and anxiety, or merely to appreciate the wonders of the natural environment.

Family Reporters ❭

Children will practice making surveys to collect data, a math skill that will foster learning about graphs and making comparisons.

 Talk Like Mathematicians!

- **Compare**—to look at two or more things closely to see what is similar or different about them
- **Gathering data**—collecting information about a specific question
- **Graph**—a diagram that shows a system of relationships among things. Graphs are also known as charts
- **Survey**—to ask many people a question or a series of questions to gather information about what most people do or think about something

How to Do It

💡 Tip: In advance, using the chart paper, create premade surveys for your child with the pictures of every member of your family. Precut an image to represent the question your child wants to ask, then place an image that represents the answer.

1. Begin by asking your child if she would like to become the family reporter to learn what things family members like the most. Explain that you will be conducting a survey with family members (for additional fun, include grandparents). Explain that mathematicians use surveys to help them find out what people really like.

2. Engage your child in a conversation about what she would like to learn. "Do you want to learn about our family's favorite fruit?" You could also find out a favorite flavor of ice cream or activity. Once you decide on the specific question to ask, you are ready to start your survey and collect the information.

3. Once you and your child have collected responses, ask, "Which column has the most images? How can we find out?" Invite your child to count each column to find out which column has more or less.

4. Encourage your child's curiosity: Find other things you could conduct a survey about. What do you think would be the family's favorite pet? A cat or a dog?

5. Encourage your child's critical-thinking skills: What can we do to find out our family's favorite pet?

Predict and Hypothesize

- Problem solve with your child: Do you think we could find out how many people in our family like dogs?
- Predict and hypothesize the answer to the question. Test the hypothesis and record what you discover.

Add more STEAM activities:

Science—What is the family's favorite plant?

Technology—What is my family's favorite technology?

Engineering—What is my family's favorite simple machine?

Pattern Adventures ❯

Introduce the concept of pattern design to help your child learn a foundational skill upon which many mathematical concepts are based. Practice identifying, designing, repeating, and extending patterns, which will build math readiness.

 ## Talk Like Mathematicians!

- **Patterns**—arrangements of things that repeat in a logical order

How to Do It

1. Ask your child to find patterns you see every day, such as the pattern of the kitchen floor or the stripes on a shirt. Look around the house for familiar patterns to observe and notice.
2. Precut some ingredients to have available for your child to explore. Explain to your child that you will be creating your own pattern in the kitchen using different ingredients.
3. Invite your child to lay out the fruit or ingredient in a pattern (banana, grape, orange), and repeat the pattern.
4. Encourage your child's curiosity: What do you think makes a pattern?
5. Encourage your child's critical-thinking skills: What can we do to find out what comes first? Which ingredient will come next?

Predict and Hypothesize

- Problem solve with your child: I wonder if we could find out how to repeat the same pattern three times.
- Predict and hypothesize the answer to the question. Test the hypothesis and record what you discover.

Add more STEAM activities:

Science—Find patterns in nature.
Technology—Find patterns in technology.
Engineering—Create your own pattern with blocks.
Arts—Find patterns in the arts.

How Far Will It Go? ❯

Compare how far objects move to further children's understanding of distance and related measurements.

 ## Talk Like Mathematicians (and Scientists)!

- **Count**—to add people or things together to find the total number
- **Distance**—the amount of space between two places or things
- **Measure**—to find out the size, length, or amount of something

- **Ramp**—inclined plane; a simple machine that increases the speed or push of an object
- **Slope**—to have a downward or upward slant

How to Do It

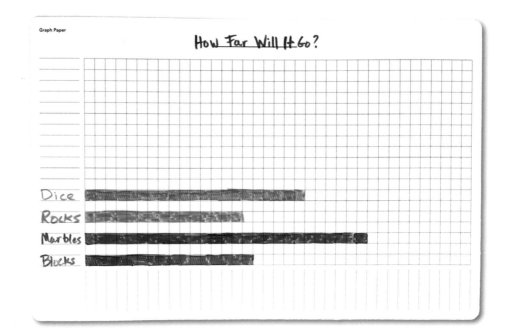

1. Tell your child that you will be conducting an investigation into how far marbles, rocks, balls, and other items will go.
2. Count the number of squares in the graphing mat.
3. Using the graphing mat as a reference, roll objects down the ramp, and mark the place where the object stopped.
4. Use blocks to build different slopes for your ramps. You can also use a plastic shoebox to increase the height of your ramp.
5. Encourage your child's curiosity: How far do you think this object will go? Try the marble, dice, and all the other objects.
6. Encourage your child's critical-thinking skills: Once the object has moved, ask, "How can we find out how far it goes? We measure the distance."

Predict and Hypothesize
- Problem solve with your child: What would happen if we increased the slope of the ramp?
- Predict and hypothesize the answer to the question. Test the hypothesis and record what you discover.

Add more STEAM activities:

Science—Go on a living and nonliving things scavenger hunt.

Technology—Use a stopwatch when the object starts rolling and mark the time when the object stops.

Engineering—Find out the source of energy for toys that move.

Arts—Use the book *Alexander and the Wind-Up Mouse* by Leo Lionni as a reference to spark creativity in designing your own toy that moves.

Sequence Adventures ❯

Introduce the concept of ordering and sequencing by organizing and arranging sets of objects. You will want to keep this very basic for younger children. It takes a lot of practice to master the concept as it is very abstract.

Talk Like Mathematicians!

- **Sequence**—a series of objects, activities, or events that occur in a logical order. Examples of sequences include the following:
  - Big, bigger, biggest
  - First, next, last
  - First, second, last
  - Long, longer, longest
  - Short, shorter, shortest
  - Small, medium, large
  - Small, smaller, smallest
  - Tall, taller, tallest

What You Need

- Precut pictures of events (what happens first, second, and third)
- Pictures of life cycles
- Sequencing mats
- Items that represent big, bigger, and biggest (blocks, crayons, toys, balls, cloths)
- Items that represent short and long (sticks or straws)
- Pictures that represent big or small, short or long
- STEAM journal

How to Do It

1. Engage your child by asking, "Who is the tallest person in the house? The shortest?"
2. Explain to your child that you will be playing a game to find out how to order different things. Start by incorporating sequencing words into your daily routines to describe the arrangement of things. Show objects to your child that illustrate big, bigger, and biggest.
3. Add more objects to introduce different concepts such as tall, taller, and tallest, and short, shorter, and shortest.
4. Encourage your child's curiosity: In a story or sequence of your choice, ask your child what would happen first, second, third.
5. Encourage your child's critical-thinking skills: The books you read provide ample opportunities to practice sequencing skills. Let your child practice critical-thinking skills by asking to predict what happens next during reading time.

Predict and Hypothesize

- Problem solve with your child: What could we make sequences of from big, bigger, and biggest around the house?
- Predict and hypothesize the answer to the question. Test the hypothesis and record what you discover.

Add more STEAM activities:

Science—Put natural things in order.

Technology—Use a story app to sequence different events for a story.

Engineering—Create structures of different sizes to compare using blocks.

Arts—Create an original artwork using leaves of different sizes.

Measurement Hunts ❯

Introduce the concept of measurement in a fun way, using your child's foot as a nonstandard measuring unit.

Talk Like Mathematicians!

- **Length**—the distance from one end of something to the other
- **Measure**—to find out the size, length, or amount of something
- **Nonstandard units**—measurements that aren't typically used, such as a pencil, an arm, and so on
- **Standard units**—widely agreed-upon measurements, such as inches, feet, and liters
-

How to Do It

1. Begin a discussion with your child about different objects used for measuring.
2. Explain to your child that you need a measurement tool in order to find out the length of things. Talk about how when we compare the size of something, we are beginning to measure it.
3. Lay out your paper and trace your child's footprint.
4. Demonstrate and explain the safe and proper use of scissors.
5. Have your child practice using scissors by having her cut out her paper foot.
6. Find different objects to measure around the house and place them on a small bag.
7. Compare and sort by size. Ask your child to measure and arrange the items in order of size.
8. Encourage your child's curiosity: What object/item do you think is biggest?
9. Encourage your child's critical-thinking skills: Can we measure with different things? Engage your child in a conversation about things we can use to measure, such as hands, crayons, Unifix cubes, and rulers. Explain the difference between standard and nonstandard units.

Predict and Hypothesize

- Problem solve with your child: Could order the items we have gathered by size?
- Predict and hypothesize the answer to the question. Test the hypothesis and record what you discover.

Add more STEAM activities:

Science—Find out the size of objects in nature.

Technology—Develop your fine motor skills by practicing scissor technology.

Engineering—Use the book *How Big is a Foot?* by Rold Myller as inspiration for designing your own shoe.

Arts—Color or paint the foot cutouts.

The Shapes of Things

Provide your child with hands-on experiences to learn the physical characteristics of shapes.

 ## Talk Like Mathematicians!

- **Circle**—a perfectly round shape; a line that is curved so that its ends meet and every point on the line is the same distance from the center
- **Rectangle**—a shape with four right angles in which one pair of parallel lines is longer than the other pair
- **Shape**—the form of an object
- **Square**—a shape that is made up of four straight sides that are the same length and four right angles
- **Triangle**—a shape that is made up of three lines and three angles

What You Need

- Books
- Objects with solid shapes (balls, boxes, cans)
- Materials of your choice (sticks, playdough)
- STEAM journal

How to Do It

1. Begin by asking your child, "How can we find shapes around the house?" Show your child everyday objects and discuss the different characteristics of shapes.
2. Invite your child to manipulate and create shapes using the materials of your choice. You may want to go online to show her examples of various shapes that she can make on her own.
3. Encourage your child's curiosity: How could you create a triangle?
4. Encourage your child's critical-thinking skills: How can we find a shape inside the shape?

Predict and Hypothesize

- Problem solve with your child: I wonder if we could create art using shapes?
- Predict and hypothesize the answers to the questions. Test the hypothesis and record what you discover.

Add more STEAM activities:

Science—Find out the shape of objects in nature.

Technology—Take a photograph of your shape.

Engineering—Use the book *The Shape of Things* by Dayle Ann Doods to design and create a prototype of a new invention.

Arts—Create art using different shapes.

References

Adams, Karlyn. 2005. *The Sources of Innovation and Creativity.* Washington, DC: National Center on Education and the Economy.

Casner-Lotto, Jill and Linda Barrington. 2006. *Are They Really Ready to Work? Employers' Perspectives on the Basic Knowledge and Applied Skills of New Entrants to the 21st Century US Workforce.* The Conference Board, Corporate Voices for Working Families, Partnership for 21st Century Skills, and the Society for Human Resource Management. New York: The Conference Board. http://files.eric.ed.gov/fulltext/ED519465.pdf

Englehart, Deirdre, et al. 2016. *STEM Play: Integrating Inquiry into Learning Centers.* Lewisville, NC: Gryphon House.

Klayman, Douglas. 2006. *Executive Summary of the Final Evaluation Report for Fairfax Pages Professional Development Project: An Effective Strategy for Improving School Readiness.* Potomac, MD: Social Dynamics.

Ludwig, Meredith, Beth Mary Marklein, and Song Mengli. 2016. *Arts Integration: A Promising Approach to Improving Early Learning.* Washington, DC: American Institutes for Research.

National Scientific Council on the Developing Child. 2007. *The Science of Early Childhood Development: Closing the Gap Between What We Know and What We Do.* Cambridge, MA Author Availible at www.developingchild.harvard.edu

National Scientific Council on the Developing Child. 2004. *Young Children Develop in an Environment of Relationships.* Working Paper No. 1. Cambridge, MA Author Availible at www.developingchild.harvard.edu/resources/wp1/

Nickerson, Raymond S. 1999. "Enhancing Creativity." In Robert J. Sternberg's *Handbook of Creativity.* Cambridge, UK: Cambridge University Press.

Sternberg, Robert J. and Linda A. O'Hara. 1999. "Creativity and Intelligence." *Handbook of Creativity.* Cambridge, UK: Cambridge University Press.

Sternberg, Robert J. 2000. "Creativity as a Decision," *Teaching for Intelligence II.* Arlington Heights, IL: Skylight Training and Publishing Inc.

Sternberg, Robert J. 2003. "Creative Thinking in the Classroom." *Scandinavian Journal of Educational Research* 47(3):325-338.

Index